CURRENT ENGLISH TWO

Shinasa

머 리 말

*Current English Two*는 현대영어로 쓰여진 글들을 한데 모은 것이다. 언제부터인지는 확실하지 않지만 Current English하면 시사영어를 가리키는 것으로 인식되고 있다. 시사(時事)는 current affairs, events, problems, questions, topics 등을 옮긴 것이므로 시사영어는 그래서 정치, 사회, 경제, 문화등의 여러 분야에서 일어나고 있는 일을 다룬 영어로 알려지고 있다. 쉽게 말해서 *Time, Newsweek, USA Today* 같은 일간지, 주간지에 실리는 기사, 논설문을 시사영어라고 보는 것이 통념으로 되어 있는 것이다.

이 용법이 틀린 것은 아니지만, 다소 한정적이라고 할 수 있다. 왜냐하면 위에서 말한 시사영어는 사실에 관한 기술이나 논의만을 포함하기 때문이다. 그러나 current라는 말은 the current month(이달)라는 말이 말해 주듯이 「지금, 이 시간에 일어나고 있는」(passing in time, or belonging to the present time) 등의 시간과 관련된 말이다. 그렇게 본다면 Current English는 비소설의 산문(non-fiction prose)만을 가리키는 것이 아니고, 현재의 영어로 쓰여진 소설, 시, 희곡도 적당히 포함할 수 있는 것이다.

이러한 시각에서 *Current English Two*는 Part 1에 많은 story를 실었다. 이것들은 문장형식으로 말하자면 이야기 narrative라고 할 수 있고, 내용은 넓은 뜻에서 미국사회에 관한 것이다. Part 2에서는 "Fenstad's Mother"가 최근에 쓰여진 단편 short story이고, 나머지는 풍자적인 유머리스트 humorist로 유명한 Art Buchwald의 글이다. 이것도 모두 미국문화와 사회에 관한 이야기이지만, 익살과 풍자를 곁들인 문장인 만큼 매우 재미있는 읽을거리가 되리라 믿는다. Part 3에 실린 글은 주로 신문, 잡지 등에 실린 「시사영어」이다. 개인적인 메시지를 비롯하여 연설문도 있고 인터뷰도 있고 설명, 서술, 토론 형식의 문장도 있다. 여기서는 가급적 다양한 문체의 산문을 제시하되 젊은 세대의 독자들이 공감할만한 내용을 담은 글을 실었다.

각주(footnote)는 인명, 지명, 책명 등의 고유명사와 다소 어려운 단어나 어구와 문법 사항의 풀이를 필요한 대목에 붙였다. 되도록 넉넉하게 붙였으므로 사전을 찾아보지 않고서도 읽어나갈 수 있으리라고 믿는다. 「시사영어」를 「공부」하면서 동시에 글읽기의 재미를 한껏 느낄 수 있기를 바라마지 않는다.

편저자

CONTENTS

PART I

PART Ⅱ

PART Ⅲ

PART I

1. The Tail of the Lobo

By *Penny Porter*

I HAD JUST FINISHED washing the lunch dishes when the screen door[1] slammed and Becky, my three-year-old, rushed in. "Mommy!" she cried. "Come see[2] my new doggy![3] I gave him water two times already. He's so thirsty!"

I sighed. Another of Becky's imaginary dogs[4]. After our old dog died, our remote home — Singing Valley Ranch in Sonoita, Ariz. — had become a lonely place for Becky. We planned to buy a puppy, but in the meantime "pretend" puppies[5] popped up everywhere.

"Please come, Mommy," Becky said, her brown eyes enormous[6].

"He's crying, and he can't walk."

Now, that was a twist[7]? All her previous make-believe dogs could do marvelous tricks. Why suddenly a dog that couldn't walk?

"All right, honey," I said. But Becky had disappeared into the mesquite by the time I followed.

"Over here by the oak stump. Hurry, Mommy!" she called. I parted the

---

1) screen door : 방충망을 유리 대신 댄 문.
2) doggy : 개(어린이 말로)
3) Come see : Come and see 또는 come to see.
4) Another ~ dogs : 또 Becky가 상상으로 만들어 낸 게군!
5) "pretend" puppies = imaginary puppies.
6) her brown eyes enormous : 갈색의 눈이 커다래져서.
7) that was a twist : 그것은 이상했다.

thorny branches and raised my hand to shade my eyes from the desert sun. A numbing chill gripped me.

There she was, sitting on her heels,[1] and cradled in her lap was the unmistakable head of a wolf! Beyond the head rose massive black shoulders. The rest of the body lay completely hidden inside the hollow stump of a fallen oak.

"Becky." My mouth felt dry. "Don't move." I stepped closer. Pale-yellow eyes narrowed. Black lips tightened, exposing double sets of two-inch fangs. Suddenly the wolf trembled, and a piteous whine rose from his throat.

"It's awright,[2] boy" crooned Becky. "Don't be afraid. That's my mommy, and she loves you too."

Then the unbelievable happened. As her tiny hands stroked the great shaggy head, I heard the gentle thump, thump, thumping[3] of the wolf's tail from deep inside the stump.

What was wrong with the animal? Why couldn't he get up? Of course.[4] Could it be rabies? Hadn't Becky said, "He's so thirsty"? My memory flashed back to[5] the five skunks who last week had torn the burlap from a leaking pipe in a frenzied effort to reach water during the final agonies of rabies.

I had to get Becky away. "Honey." My throat tightened. "Put-his-head-down-and-come- to- Mommy.[6] We'll go find help."[7]

Becky got up, kissed the wolf on the nose and walked slowly to my outstretched arms. Sad yellow eyes followed her. Then the wolf's head sank

---

1) sitting on her hills : 뒤꿈치를 깔고 앉아서. 즉 무릎을 꿇고 앉아서.
2) awright = all right
3) thump, thump, thumping : 텅, 텅, 텅 치는 소리. ing 가 마지막에 붙은 것은 thump, thump, thump를 한개의 동사로 본 것이기 때문임.
4) Of course! : 틀림없이 그거야. 즉 광견병 때문일 것이라는 뜻.
5) My memory flashed back to : ~이 퍼뜩 떠올랐다.
6) Put~Mommy : -으로 단어들을 연결한 것은 그것들을 한 단어같이 이어서 또박또박 말한 것을 나타냄.
7) go find help = go and (or to) find help.

to the ground.

With Becky safe in my arms[1)] I ran to my car parked by the house and sped to the barns where Jake, one of the cowhands, was saddling up. "Jake. come quickly. Becky found a wolf in the oak stump near the wash. I think it has rabies."

Back at the house[2)] I put my tearful child down for her nap. "But I want to give my doggy his water," she cried. I kissed her and gave her some stuffed animals to play with. "Let Mommy and Jake take care of him for now"[3)] I said.

Moments later I reached the oak stump. Jake stood looking down at the beast. "It's a Mexican lobo, all right,[4)] he said, "and a big one!" The wolf whined, and then we both caught the smell of gangrene.

"When! It's not rabies," Jake said. "But he's sure[5)] hurt bad. Shall I put him out of his misery?"[6)]

The word "yes" was on my lips, but never spoken. Becky emerged from the bushes. "Is Jake going to make him well?[7)] Mommy?" She hauled the beast's head into her lap once more. She buries her face in the coarse, dark fur. This time I wasn't the only one who heard the thumping echo of the lobo's tail.

That afternoon my husband, Bill, and our veterinarian came to see the wolf. Observing the trust the animal had in our child, Doc said to me, "Suppose[8)] you let Becky and me tend to this fella[9)] together. Minutes later, as

---

1) With~ arms : 부대상황, 즉, Becky가 안전하게 내 품에 안기자.
2) Back at the house : 집으로 돌아 와서.
3) for now : 지금은.
4) all right : 확실히, 분명히.
5) sure = surely.
6) Shall~ misery ? : 즉, 죽인다는 뜻임.
7) make him well : 그를 낫게 하다.
8) Suppose ~ : ~하면 어떨까.
9) tend~ fella : 이 녀석을 돌보다. fella = fellow.

child and vet reassured the stricken beast, the hypodermic found its mark.[1] The yellow eyes closed.

"He's asleep now," said the vet. "Give me a hand here,[2] Bill." They pulled the massive body out of the stump. The animal must have been five and a half feet long,[3] and well over 100 pounds. The hip and leg had been mutilated by bullets. Doc peeled away the rotten flesh. He dug out bone splinters, cleaned the wound and gave a dose of penicillin. Next day he returned and inserted a metal rod, replacing the missing bone.[4]

"Well, it looks like you've got yourselves a Mexican lobo[5]." Doc said. "They don't tame real easy.[6] I'm amazed at the way this fella took to you little gal."[7]

Becky named the wolf Ralph, and carried food and water to the stump every day. Ralph's recovery was not easy. For three months he dragged his injured hindquarters by clawing the earth with his front paws. From the way[8] he lowered his eyelids when we massaged the atrophied limbs, we knew he endured excruciating pain, but not once did he ever try[9] to bite the hands of those who cared for him.

Four months to the day,[10] Ralph finally stood unaided. His huge frame shook as long-unused muscles[11] were activated. Bill and I patted and praised him. But it was Becky to whom he turned for[12] a gentle word, a kiss,

---

1) the hypodermic found its mark : 피하주사 (즉 마취제)가 제대로 놓아졌다.
2) Give~ here : 이것 좀 도와주게.
3) must ~ long : 이때의 must는 ~임이 틀림없다의 뜻. must have been은 그것의 과거형임.
4) the missing bone : 없어진 뼈.
5) it looks ~ lobo : 당신 멕시코 늑대 한 마리 생긴 것 같아.
6) don't tame real easy : 길들이기가 어렵다.
7) at the way ~ gal : 이녀석이 당신 딸을 좋아하는 것을 보고.
8) From the way : ~하는 것을 보아 (판단할 때에).
9) not once ~ try ~ : not once를 강조해서 문두에 둠으로써 주어 동사가 도치되었음.
10) Four months to the day : 꼭 네 달만에.
11) long ~ unused muscles = muscles that had been long unused.
12) turned for ~ : turn to someone for something은 "누구에게서 무엇을 바라다"의 뜻.

or a smile. He responded to these gestures of love by swinging his great bushy tail like a pendulum.

As his strength grew, Ralth followed Becky all over the ranch. Together they roamed the desert pastures, the golden-haired child often stooping low, sharing with the great lame wolf whispered[1] secrets of nature's wonders. When evening came, he would[2] return like a silent shadow to his hollow stump.

As he wandered the ranch, Ralph never chased the cattle. However, his excessive drooling when I let my chickens run loose[3] prompted my husband to build a fenced-in poultry yard.

And what a watchdog he was! Feral dogs and coyotes became only memories[4] at Singing Valley Ranch. Ralph was king.

Becky's first day of school was sad for Ralph. When the bus left, he refused to return to the yard. Instead, he lay by the side of the road and waited. When Becky returned, he limped and tottered in wild, joyous circles around her[5]. This welcoming ritual remained unchanged throughout her school years.

Although Ralph seemed happy on the ranch, he disappeared into the Santa Catalina Mountains for several weeks during the spring mating season, leaving us to worry about his safety. This was calving season,* and fellow ranchers watched for the coyote, the cougar and, of course, the lone wolf. But Ralph was lucky.

Year after year we wondered about his mate, and the pups he

---

1) the golden-haired child~ wonders : 부대상황. whipered secrets of nature's wonder는 sharing의 목적어임.
2) would : 과거의 습관을 나타냄.
3) let my chickens run loose : 닭들을 풀어 놓았다.
4) became only memories : 단지 옛날 일이 되었다.
5) in wild ~ her : 흥분하고, 좋아서 그녀 주위를 돌며.

undoubtedly sired.[1] We learned that the wolf retruns to his mate to help feed the young. We wondered how much of Ralph's own food he dragged off to his hidden family. Each June, Becky gave him extra food because he grew so thin.

During Ralph's 12 years on our ranch, the habits of his life became rituals,[2] and his love for our child never wavered. At last the spring came when he returned home with another bullet wound. The day after Ralph's injury, some ranchers whose land bordered ours told us they'd got a big she-wolf. The mate had been shot at also, but he kept running.

Becky was 15 years old now. She sat with Ralph's head resting on her lap. He, too, must have been about 15 and was gray with age. As Bill removed the bullet, my memory spun back through the years. Once again I saw a chubby three-tear-old stroking the head of a huge black wolf.

The wound wasn't serious, but Ralph didn't get well. Precious pounds fell away,[3] and his trips to the yard in search of Becky's loving companionship ceased. All day long he rested quietly.

But when night fell, old and stiff as he was, he disappeared into the hills. And each morning his food was gone.

The day came when we found him dead in front of the oak stump. The yellow eyes were closed. A lump in my throat choked me[4] as I watched Becky stroke his shaggy neck, tears streaming down her face.[5] "I'll miss him so," she cried.

As I covered him with a blanket, we were startled by a strange rustling sound from inside the stump. Becky looked inside. Two tiny yellow eyes

---

1) the pups ~ sired : 그가 분명 낳게 한 새끼들. undoubtedly는 그가 새끼를 친 것이 분명하다는 뜻.
2) become rituals : 여기서 의식은 어김없이 일어나는 일이라는 뜻임.
3) Precious pounds fell away : 한 파운드가 소중한 처지에 체중이 떨어졌다. precious = irreplaceable or irretrievable.
4) A lump ~ me : 목이 메었다.
5) tears~face : 부대상황. 즉 눈물이 얼굴에 흘러 내리는 가운데에.

peered back, and puppy fangs glinted in the semi-darkness. Ralph's pup.[1] The motherless pup,[2] he had tried to care for alone.

Had a dying instinct told Ralph his offspring would be safe here, as he had been, with those who loved him. Hot tears spilled on baby fur as Becky gathered the trembling bundle in her arms.

"It's all right, little... Ralphie" she murmured. "Don't be afraid. That's my mom, and she loves you too."

Did I hear a distant echo then? A gentle thump, thump, thumping — the tail of the Lobo?

---

1) Ralph's pup = It was Ralph's pup.
2) The motherless pup : 뒤의 care for의 목적어임.

2. Unsolved Mysteries of the Incas

By *Ronald Schiller*

Perched between two lofty peaks above the Urubamba River in the Peruvian Andes stands the breathtakingly beautiful Inca city of Machu Picchu[1] with its houses, courtyards and shrines – one of the most extraordinary archeological sites on earth.[2] Until its discovery by the American explorer Hiram Bingham in 1911, it lay empty and almost forgotten for nearly five centuries. For reasons unknown,[3] sometime during the 15th or 16th century the city was abandoned.

Still another mystery is how the Incas constructed the massive stone buildings at Machu Picchu and elsewhere without draft animals,[4] wheeled vehicles or iron tools. All they had were stone hammers, bronze chisels, bronze and wooden crowbars, and fiber ropes.[5] Yet with these primitive tools they split granite blocks and hauled them on wooden rollers up deep gorges[6] to building sites sometimes miles away. Then, using no mortar[7] they fitted them together so tightly that it is impossible to insert a knife

---

1) Perched~Machu Picchu~ : Perched~Andes는 동사 stands의 보어. 이 문장의 주어는 the breathtakingly beautiful Inca city of Machu Picchu임.
2) one of~earth : Machu Picchu와 동격임.
3) For reasons unknown : 알 수 없는 이유로.
4) draft animals : 짐 끄는 동물.
5) fiber ropes : (식물의) 섬유로 만든 밧줄.
6) up deep gorges : 경사가 급한 골짜기 위로.
7) using no mortar : without using mortar.

blade between them.

Such engineering marvels abound in Inca land. Sacsahuaman, the cyclopean fortress[1] guarding the capital, Cuzco, is constructed of[2] many-sided boulders weighing over 300 tons each. These enormous stones had to be lifted, lowered, and their edges ground down with sand and water[3] until they achieved a perfect fit.

The Incas, whose empire flourished very late in the history of Peru, inherited their skills from earlier, much different cultures. One of these dates back to[4] 851 B.C., and revolved around[5] a ceremonial center deep in the central Andes called Chavín de Huantar. An eerie place,[6] the stone walls of its temples are embellished with nightmare friezes of ferocious feline demons[7] with writhing snakes in place of hair.[8]

A militaristic yet highly religious culture evolved around A.D. 300 in the Moche Valley on the north coast of Peru. The people here erected one of the most massive structures ever raised by man: a pyramid 1000 feet long by 520 feet wide, built of more than 140 million clay bricks. Now a vandalized ruin,[9] it must have been a dazzling sight in its glory,[10] 100 feet high and covered with brilliant murals.

Fifteen-hundred year old Mochica ceramic vessels portray[11] snobbish

---

1) the cyclopean fortress : 거대한 성새. Sacsahuaman과 동격임.
2) of : 자료를 나타냄.
3) ground~ water : 물에 축인 모래로 갈아 낸.
4) dates back to ~ : 연대가 ~까지 거슬러 올라간다.
5) revolved around ~ : ~을 중심으로 하였다.
6) An eerie place : 위의 a ceremonial center~ Huantar와 동격. "기이한 곳으로서. 그곳 사원의 석벽들은 ~" 식으로 번역함이 좋음.
7) nightmare ~demons : 고양이 형상을 한 사나운 악마들이 새겨진 악몽같은 프리즈들.
8) with~hair : 머리칼 대신에 꿈틀거리는 뱀이 달린.
9) Now a vandalized ruin : 지금은 파괴된 폐허인. vandalize는 5세기경 로마와 구라파를 침략한 게르만족의 하나인 Vandal족에서 유래하는 말로, 이들은 특히 문화재를 약탈하고 파괴한 야만적 행동으로 유명함.
10) in its glory : 전성기에는.
11) Fifteen~portray~ : ~들이 1500년 전에 만들어진 Mochica의 자기 그릇에 그려져 있다.

nobles, cringing beggars, and men whose noses had been cut off (possibly as punishment for crimes), as well as surprisingly explicit sexual scenes. Unsurpassed brocades and tapestries were intricately embroidered with feathers, gold and turquoise woven into the fabric[1], some displaying as many as 190 different hues.

Next came the legendary stone city of Tiahuanaco, one-time capital of an empire that flourished on the Bolivian side of Lake Titicaca between A.D. 600 and 1100. At an elevation of some 14,000 feet[2], it is one of the most dramatic sites in the Andes.

Around A.D. 1000, the kingdom of Chimor arose on the north coast of Peru. Its capital, Chanchan, eight square miles in area, may have been one of the largest and wealthiest cities in the world at that time. One of the few pre-Columbian cities whose end we know,[3] it fell to the conquering Incas[4] around 1467. Only vestiges remain of the brilliant friezes[5] that covered its plastered walls.

Incredibly, the Peruvians achieved their great cultures without a written language and with no currency. Trade was entirely by barter. (Precious metals were sacred, with gold, regarded as "the sweat of the sun[6]," to be used only for religious purposes or by the emperor and nobility.)

The origin of Peruvian cultural arts remains largely a matter of hypotheses.[7] Some evidence — such as the appearance around 200 B.C. of pottery figurines similar to those of eastern Asia —suggests trans-Pacific influence.[8]

---

1) embroidered~fabric : 천에 넣어 짠 깃털과 금과 터키옥으로 아롱진.
2) At~ feet : 해발 약 1,400피트 되는 고지에.
3) the few~ know : 그 후를 우리가 아는, 몇 안되는 Columbus(의 발견) 이전의 도시들.
4) it~Incas : 그 도시는 정복자인 잉카족에 함락됐다.
5) of the brilliant friezes ~ : of 이하는 의미상으로 앞의 vestiges에 걸림.
6) with~sun : 금은 "태양의 땀"으로 여겨지는 등.
7) remains~hypotheses : 아직도 대부분은 가설로 남아있다. 즉, 아직 잘 모른다는 뜻.
8) trans-Pacific influence : 태평양 너머로부터 온 영향.

However, given the same[1] problems, materials and opportunities, widely separated peoples often come up with[2] similar solutions: and if there had been transoceanic contact, the Peruvians surely should have acquired the idea of a written language and learned the use of the wheel. Still, there are intriguing questions. Why should panpipes, tuned to the same pitch, using the same musical scale[3] turn up[4] both in South America and the Western Pacific? Why should sixth-century Peruvian vases portray apparently Oriental faces, while others bear the features of Africans and Arabs?

Among the world's most intriguing archeological finds are the gigantic geometric designs and figures of birds, animals and insects inscribed on the plains of Nazca, near Peru's southern coast.[5] Most of them were "drawn" some 1400 years ago by removing some of the dark-colored stones that pave the desert to expose[6] in patterns, the light-colored clay beneath. Far too large to be reconizable at ground level[7], the figures were not widely known until 1939, when a historian discovered the figure of a huge bird while mapping ancient irrigation ditches.

Flying-saucer enthusiasts claim the lines and geometic figures were navigational aids and landing strips[8] for ancient spaceships, but a more plausible explanation is offered by science : the crisscrossing lines may be markers pointing to positions of sun, moon and stars at significant times of the year; the animal figures may represent constellations. The Nazcans could have associated a rising water level in the river on which they depended for irrigation with[9] the appearance of the Monkey constellation

---

1) given the same ~ : 같은~ 이 주어 질 경우.
2) come up with~ : ~을 안출해내다.
3) using the same musical scale : 같은 음계를 사용하는.
4) turn up : 나타나다, 출현하다.
5) Among~ coast : 도치된 문장. 주부는 the gigantic~coast임.
6) to expose : 목적을 나타내는 부정사로 위의 removing에 걸림.
7) Far~level : 지면에 서서 알아 보기에는 너무 커서.
8) navigational~strips : 항행을 위한 보조물과 활주로.
9) with ~ : 위의 associated a rising water level에 걸림.

(part of our Big Dipper) ; drawing its image on the ground in such a large scale may have been a way of ensuring the constellation's return.

The Incas themselves shrouded their origins in myth and legend. Their emperor claimed to be a descendant of the sun god. What we do know is that they founded their capital in Cuzco around A.D. 1100 and struggled for decades with warring tribes around them. Then, in 1438, they burst out of the city. By the time the Spanish arrived in 1532, they ruled a vast empire stretching 2500 miles from the border of modern Colombia in the north, halfway down the coast of Chile in the south, and eastward deep in to Bolivia and northern Argentina.

The Incas developed an amazing social structure, probably one of[1] the most regimented, workaholic welfare states[2] the world has ever known. The population was'divided into 12 age groups, each assigned specific duties.[3] Every able-bodied male served in the army and worked on public roads.[4] Crops were divided among church, state and community, and there was always an ample amount stored to supply the army and to meet emergencies. If earthquakes, floods or other calamities occurred, necessities poured in from other provinces.[5]

Nobody lacked food, clothing or shelter, but nobody enjoyed much freedom either. The people were told where to live[6] : what crops to plant, how to dress, whom to marry. Surprise inspections called see-alls[7] were made by officials. Lying, laziness and adultery were punishable by death. The most attractive young girls, the Chosen Women, were selected to spend

---

1) probably one of ～ : which was probably one of ～.
2) welfare states : 복지국가들.
3) each assigned specific duties = and each (group) was assigned specific duties
4) worked ～ roads : 공공도로를 만들거나 보수하는 작업을 했다.
5) necessities～ provinces : 다른 (즉 재해를 당하지 않은) 지방으로부터 생필품이 쏟아져 들어왔다.
6) The people～live : 사람들은 사는 장소를 지정 받았다.
7) surprise～see-alls : 일체검사라고 불리는 예고 또는 검열.

cloistered lives[1] as "Virgins of the Sun."

Impossible as it may seem, the Incas managed their vast empire without a written language or numerals. Messages were sent to the capital by word of mouth[2], relayed via an extensive road network by fleet-footed runners called *chasquis*, and committed to memory[3] by professional *camayocs* (rememberers). All accounts were kept on *quipus*, collections of long, knotted strings of various lengths and colors that recorded statistics. With information provided by *quipus*, *chasquis* and *camayocs*, the Incas could muster armies of thousands from various parts of the empire in a matter of days[4], and supply them with known quantites[5] of weapons and food for months at a time.

That this superbly organized empire could be overthrown in 1532 by 170 Spanish adventurers was due largely to coincidence. Francisco Pizarro and his men arrived at the end of a disastrous five year civil war over succession to the Inca throne[6] that had decimated the armies and left the government a shambles.[7] Split into dissident factions, some Incas joined the invaders. When the emperor Atahualpa entered the Spanish camp near Cajamarca at the invitation of the Spaniards, he was seized by Pizarro, and thousands of his men were slaughtered. Finally realizing that the Spaniards were after the precious metals, Atahualpa promised to fill the large room in which he stood halfway to the roof[8] — once with gold, and twice again[9] with silver —if they would release him. Althogh he kept his part of the bargain, the Spanish

1) cloistered lives : 경내를 벗어나지 못하는 생활.
2) by word of mouth : 구두를 통한 말로.
3) committed to memory : 암기되었다.
4) in a matter of days : 며칠 안에.
5) known quantities : 파악된 양의.
6) over~throne : Inca의 왕위 계승에 관한.
7) left~shambles : 조정을 아수라장으로 만들어 놓은.
8) in which~root : 천정까지의 높이가 그의 키의 두배가 되는.
9) twice again : 그만큼의 두 배를.

strangled him anyway.

With its god-king gone[1], the paralyzed empire disintegrated. It was a tragedy from which Peru has not yet recovered, and an irreplaceable cultural loss to the world.

1) With its god-king gone : 신과 같은 군왕이 없어지자.

3. Where Have All the Fathers Gone?

By *Lester Velie*

Becoming a father is easy. *Being* a father[1] is difficult. Ask these fathers. They know :

Commuter : Bruce M, a young advertising executive, rises at 6 a.m. while his two toddlers are still abed. He travels 30 miles to his New York City office and returns about 7 p.m. When a big ad campaign is being mapped,[2] he may return as late as 10 p.m. On many weekdays, the most he can do as a father is to look wistfully at his sleeping children before and after work. Weekends? Every other Saturday or so, Bruce locks himself up in his study[3] with a bulging briefcase of work—or, to escape wife and children, flees to his office. Along with millions of other young husbands who follow the commuter way of life[4], Bruce is an "invisible father."

Pawn : Bill W, father of two adolescents, is a pawn in a corporate chess game.[5] Every few years,[6] he is moved to a new square in new city by a company which considers this[7] "good for the company and for the career

1) Being a father : 아버지 노릇하기.
2) when~mapped : 큰 광고 운동을 면밀히 계획할 때는.
3) locks~study : 문을 걸고 서재 안에 들어가 있는다.
4) who~life : (교외에서 시내로) 통근하는 식의 생활을 하는.
5) is~game : 회사라고 하는 장기의 졸(卒)이다.
6) Every few years : 몇 년 만큼씩마다.
7) this : 위에 언급된 것같이 옮겨 가는 것을 뜻함.

development of the individual"[1] What this does to the development of Bill's uprooted children,[2] the company doesn't say. Of course, Bill doesn't have to move if he doesn't want to. But Bill is a willing pawn, because he believes this is the way to become a corporate knight.[3]

Good citizen : Henry S, father of two pre-adolescents, heads his town's school board.[4] He is on the board of the Community Chest[5] and is a chief money-raiser during annual fund-raising campaigns. Henry also umpires Little League[6] games and helps raise money to fight muscular dystrophy.[7] Not long ago, Henry's wife said to him, "Do you realize that you haven't been in the house for ten consecutive nights, and I haven't been out of it?"[8]

Henry's natural inclination to do good is exploited by his company, which tells its executives that such efforts are "good for our image." Unions also pressure members to "get involved."[9] and so do most people's neighbors. Result? Millions of Henrys are involved with everybody's busiess except that of their own children.

Moonlighter : Joe H, father of five, pounds a policeman's beat[10] by day and drives a cab by night to keep his family in groceries.[11] Joe has lots of company[12] especially among those who work in low-paid industries. The Labor Department tells us that some four million workers are holding down[13] two or more jobs.

---

1) for~individual : 사원의 경력을 위해서도.
2) What~children : 뒤의 say의 목적어임.
3) to become a corporate knight : 회사(라는 장기)의 기사 (즉 간부)가 되는.
4) heads his town's school board : 시교육위원회 위원장이다.
5) the Community Chest : (사회사업을 위한) 공동모금.
6) Little League : (미국의 12세 미만) 소년 야구 리그.
7) to~dystrophy : 근육의 영양실조를 방지하기 위한.
8) it : the house를 받음.
9) to "get involved" : 적극 참여하라고.
10) pounds a policeman's beat :경관으로서 자기에게 주어진 관할구역을 돌아다닌다.
11) to~ groceries : 집안 식구를 먹여살리기 위해.
12) has lots of company : 비슷한 처지의 사람이 대단히 많다.
13) hold down : 유지하다. 잘 해내다.

The kids? "That's the old lady's job."[1]

Low Man : Homer J, father of four children ranging in age from nine months to nine years is low man on the job totem pole.[2] Because of the color of his skin and his lack of salable skills, he is the last to be hired when jobs are plentiful and the first to be fired when jobs are scarce. Since the welfare laws of his state bar Aid to Families of Dependent Children[3] if there's a man around the house[4] even if unemployed, Homer has vanished so that his wife and kids can eat. With unemployment holding around five percent, there are close to a million fathers who are unable to bring home the bread — and therefore are unable to be fathers.

The father is the forgotten man of our society.

Sociologists and psychologists who turn out reams of research papers on mothers virtually ignore the father. Anti-family critics ignore him, too. They tell us the family itself is outmoded and that new models—group marriage or permissive "kiss-and-tell" marriage[5] work better. None of them suggests that the going model,[6] which has served us for centuries, would work better if only the father had more of a chance to help.

Now, however, reports are beginning to trickle in[7] that show the father's importance.

"The father's influence begins before the baby is born—by keeping the expectant mother[8] in a good frame of mind" says psychologist Henry B.

---

1) the old lady's job : 마누라의 일.
2) the job totem pole : 직업 서열.
3) Families of Dependent Children : 부양 아동이 있는 가족.
4) if~ house : 집안에 장성한 남자가 있으면.
5) "kiss-and-tell" marriage 부부가 서로 혼외정사를 솔직히 이야기하고 또 인정하는 관계.
6) the going model : 현재 통용되고 있는 모델.
7) are beginning to trickle in : 조금씩 들어오고 있다.
8) the expectant mother : 임신한 여자.

Biller of the University of Rhode Island. And it remains crucial, says Biller, even in those early years when the mother supposedly is the key parent.[1] "In fact," Biller points out, "the father is probably more important than the mother to the healthy sexual development of both boys and girls.

"The father tends to differentiate considerably more than the mother between his sons and daughters and to reward his children's sex-appropriate behavior more than she does. Thus the father-deprived child is more likely to have problems in his relations with the opposite sex — stemming from a lack of a secure sex-role orientation.[2] Studies of the family backgrounds of both male and female homosexuals reveal a very high incidence of father-deprivation."[3]

Lack of adequate fathering may damage a child's school progress,[4] too. Biller and a colleague studied 44 third-grade boys in the Cape Cod, Mass., area, whose involvement with their fathers ranged from two hours or more a day (high father presence) to less than six hours a week (low father presence). Biller reported: "The high-father-present group demonstrated a much higher level of academic achievement."

Why? Principally because, Biller believes, a warm relationship with a father fosters the self-confidence needed for achievement.

The family has the job of socializing the child, teaching him the values of the society and the rules of the game. Cornell University researchers have found, in a study of middle-class boys, that when one or both parents are frequently absent from home, adolescents are likely to turn to each other for their values.[5] Such children are more likely, said the Cornell report, to be "pessimistic about the future, rate lower in responsibility and leadership,

---

1) the key parent : 양친 중 결정적 역할을 하는 쪽.
2) a secure sex-role orientation : 확실한 성역할지도.
3) a very high incidence of father-deprivation : 부친 결손의 매우 높은 비율을.
4) school progress : 학업 발전.
5) to turn~values : 가치관 정립을 위한 도움을 서로에게서 구하다.

and are more likely to engage in anti-social behavior."

In a companion study,[1] Cornell psychologist Urie Bronfenbrenner added: "Perhap because it was more pronounced, relative absence of the father[2] was more critical than that of the mother."

Looking at evidence like this, behavioral scientists are beginning to tell us that the neglected—and neglectful —father[3] is a root cause for many of our social headaches: youth crime, drug abuse, the counterculture's rebellion against marriage and the family[4]—and, indeed, what the most recent White House Conference on Children called "a breakdown in the process of making human beings human."

To arrest[5] this breakdown we must strengthen the traditional functions of the family. This in turn[6] requires, as Prof. Lawrence E. Fuchs of Brandeis University puts it, "the restoration of father."

The American father's authority inside the family has been downgraded, Fuchs argues, because of the pressures on him from outside. Pressure on the American male begins in boyhood, when more is expected of him than of his sister,[7] continues throughout college and graduate school, and reaches a killing pace[8] in early manhood and middle age. At the turn of the century,[9] the average man died two years and ten months earlier than the average woman. Today's average male dies six years earlier than the female.

While father is killing himself to succeed[10] authority inside the family

---

1) In a companion study : 그와 함께 이루어진 연구에서.
2) relative absence of the father : (어머니에 대한) 상대적인 아버지의 부재.
3) the neglected ~ father : 경시당하는—그리고 스스로 자기 임무에 태만한—아 버지는.
4) counterculture's ~ family : 결혼과 가족(제도)에 대한 반문화의 반항. 기성 사회규범에 반대되는 가치관과 관습을 가진 문화를 반문화라고 함.
5) arrest = stop.
6) in turn : 차례로. ~나름으로.
7) when more~sister : 누이에게보다 그에게 대한 기대가 더 클 때에. of는 from의 뜻.
8) reaches~pace : 살인적인 정도에 이른다.
9) At the turn of the century : 금세기가 시작됐을 때에.
10) is killing himself to succeed : 성공하려고 필사의 노력을 경주하고 있다.

devolves to the mother. It is she who must civilize the little savages; it is she who insists that they go to bed on time and get up in time to catch the school bus ; that[1] they pick up their things, help set the table,[2] live in relative peace. And it is the mother who confers with the teacher, attends PTA meetings,[3] arranges for doctor appointments.

The authority-relinquishing father[4] does more than deprive his children of the strong hand[5] needed in their upbringing. His preoccupation elsewhere[6] may be interpreted as indifference by his children, and so stir up the bitterness that leads to alienation and rebellion.

What the American family needs most, says Fuchs, is a strong father — not an authoritarian tyrant, but a sympathetic, listening, authoritative parent. And one who is around to deliver the fathering services in person.[7]

How do we bring father back into the lives of his children? Well, for openers,[8] the father might try self-help.[9]

For instance, a young Assistant U.S. Attorney I know, Frank C, whose job often keeps him at his office nights and weekends, manages, nevertheless, to be a visible father. He invites his wife and three-year-old son to town for periodic lunches[10] and, on working weekends, takes them to his courthouse office, where the boy charges up and down the corridor on his tricycle. Or, during a break, father takes son to a nearby courtroom, sits the boy on the judge's bench and watches happily as he hammers away with a toy gavel.[11]

---

1) that～ : 위의 insist에 걸림.
2) help set the table : 밥상 보는 것을 도우라고.
3) PTA meetings : 사친회 모임. PTA = Parent Teacher Association.
4) The authority relinquishing father : 권위를 포기하는 아버지.
5) the strong hand : 엄격함.
6) elsewhere : 이 경우는 자녀교육 이외의 것을 뜻함.
7) who ～ person : 아버지로서 할 일을 실제로 수행하기 위해 늘 가까이에(즉 집안에) 있는.
8) for openers : 우선은, 첫째는.
9) try self-help : 스스로 노력해 보다.
10) for periodic lunches : 주기적으로 점심에 (초대하다).
11) hammer ～ gavel : 장난감 판결봉을 마구 두드려 댄다.

Research reveals that it isn't only the quantity of time a parent spends in the home that counts; it's also the quality of involvement with the child.

One significant and unexpected force that is at work to bring fathers into the lives of children is the recharged feminist movement. While the sisters' primary objective is, of course, to liberate the neglected mother, they are forcing us to do something about the neglected father, too.

For example: Maternity benefits are already here,[1] and more companies are adopting them, thanks to a decision by the Equal Employment Opportunity Commission that pregnancy and giving birth are a disability, to be paid for by disability insurance.[2] Now, feminists — and sociologists, too — are asking: What about "paternity benefits" as well?[3]

Sociologist Alice Rossi of Goucher College put it this way: "Some changes have to be made regarding the father's role at birth time. Perhaps the concept of sick leave[4] has to be expanded to allow a man to spend more time at home after his children are born and while they are very young."

Some American Federation of Teachers' locals[5] in New Jersey have propose parental-leave contract clauses[6] that will permit a husband a week of leave-with-pay[7] when his wife has a baby. And the International Union of Electrical, Radio and Machine Workers has a contract with Textron, Inc., at Rochester, N.Y., which permits either parent — or both — up to 18 months' leave-without-pay to care for a new child.

Perhaps if the feminists could breach that male stronghold, the company board of directors,[8] they could put still more fathers to work on fathering.

---

1) Maternity～here : 출산수당은 이미 시행되고 있다.
2) to be～ insurance : 폐질보험(廢疾保險)으로 보상되야 할.
3) What～ well? : "아버지 수당"도 만드는 것이 어떨까?
4) sick leave : 병가(病暇).
5) locals : 지회들.
6) parental～leave contract clauses : 부모노릇을 하기 위한 휴가에 대한 계약 조항.
7) leave with pay : 유급휴가.
8) breach～directors : 남성의 아성인 회사의 이사회를 뚫고 들어간다.

Inevitably, women directors would soon be asking such questions as, "Is this convention trip[1] necessary?" Or, "What, transfer young Jones again?" His kids have barely settled into their *present* school!

The White House Conference on Children reported that business and industry, more than any other institutions in our society, determine the life-style of the American family — and so have the opportunity to determine the fate of the American family and the American child.

Employers alone, of course, can't be blamed for the American phenomenon known as the "rat race."[2] The individual has his own drives, nourished by a lifetime of conditioning, to achieve. Nevertheless, there are some things the employer can do to help a man be a father.

Urie Bronfenbrenner suggests, for example, that corporations could improve their chances of attracting executive talent[3] by offering a new kind of fringe benefit[4]: more leisure for family matters, created by reducing job obligations that require absence from home on weekends and evenings. Bronfenbrenner also suggests that employers should create more part-time jobs[5] and give these jobs more status[6] — so as to permit parents to spend more time with their children.

Fathers and fathering can be restored to the American family. The first step is to reaize that healthy family life, and the health of our society, depend on it.

---

1) this convention trip : 연차 총회에 가기 위한 이번 출장.
2) rat race : 무의미한(무모한) 경쟁.
3) executive talent : 유능한 중역.
4) fringe benefit : 부수적 이득.
5) part~time job : 비상근 일자리들.
6) give~status : 이런 직업의 처우를 개선하다.

4. Is There a Substitute for God?

By *David Raphael Klein*

It is hard to say where it started. With Gutenberg? Galileo? The industrial revolution? Darwinism? Somewhere along the way,[1] Western man began to lose his belief in God as a personal force,[2] as decider of his fate, as ultimate judge of his actions. The idea that God created man become old-fashioned; we evolved.[3] The notion of Hell was picturesque, but no longer compelling. Life began to be seen as more or less accidental; sin became a relative, sociological matter, and to many a pure fiction. After millenniums of living under gods, man came to regard such belief as archaic and superstitious. Like a son who decides he need not depend upon his father any longer, he set forth to make his own way[4] in the world.

He still believed in right and wrong, and he still knew when he was doing wrong, as he saw it[5], but he no longer believed he had offended God by it[6] or incurred His punishment. In fact, there was no punishment; he only felt guilty, or resolved not to do wrong again.

The difference between living this way, and trying to live righteously

1) Somewhere along the way : 그 어간의 어디에서인가.
2) as a personal force : 구체적인 힘으로써.
3) we evolved : 우리는 (창조된 것이 아니라) 진화해서 되었다.
4) set~way : 자신의 힘으로 나아가기 시작했다.
5) as he saw it : 자기 주관대로.
6) it : 위의 doing wrong을 받음.

because God commands it is profound. A man could now do anything he wanted, subject only to[1]the laws of the land and his own judgment. Yet this judgment[2] he had formed in part from parents and institutions whose outlooks was still religious. So, although he has denied the basis of the morality of his forebears, such a man still acts in its terms.[3] He obeys the Commandments without believing they were commanded; he speaks of right and wrong in the framework of conviction he no longer possesses; he acts according to a Judeo-Christian ethic, although he has adjured the belief.

How did he manage to get into such a contradictory position?

Just as some primitive peoples have accepted Christianity by transposing their old gods onto the new religion,[4] so have many moderns transposed their inherited ethic onto another structure : the needs of society. What used to be an offense against God became "anti-social"; a sin became a crime; religious precepts governing conduct became matters of hygiene, efficiency or social value. Stealing was bad because honesty is the best policy. You tried to avoid being unfaithful to your mate because it might harm your relationship. If you attended religious services, it was to respect a tradition.[5] Virtue became its own inexplicable reward, for there was no other.[6]

A societally-based ethic[7] such as this is variable according to time, place and circumstance. There are no absolutes in it, and it has no clear, codified system. Opinion becomes the basis of the code, and the pollster the prophet.[8]

---

1) subject only to ~ : 오직 ~에만 지배받는.
2) this judgment : 뒤의 formed의 목적어.
3) in its terms : 그것에 (조상들의 도덕률에) 의해서.
4) by~religion : 그들의 옛날 신들을 새 종교(즉 기독교)에 전이 시킴으로써.
5) it~tradition : (신을 믿어서가 아니라) 전통을 존중하기 위해서이다.
6) for there was no other : 그 자체밖에는 다른 보상이 없기 때문이다. 옛날에도 Virtue is its own reward라는 말이 있었으나 그때에는 덕을 행하는 것이 신의 뜻을 따르는 것으로 생각되어서, 그것이 이승에서는 아무 보상이 없더라도 종교적인 위안과 만족감을 주었으나, 신을 부정하는 현대에서는 그마저 없어지고 순전히 덕을 행하는 기쁨 그 자체밖에는 다른 보상이 없다는 뜻.
7) A societally~based ethic = An ethic that is baced on societal needs.
8) the pollster the prophet : the pollster 다음에 becomes가 생략됐음.

It is an ethic without appreciable roots in the past[1] to reassure us, and subject to change at any time with some new event or scientific discovery — as Freudianism, for example, changed the moral outlook of so many.

Examine one possible consequence. Suppose[2] a government decided, on the basis of available data, that a new law was required which would impose the death penalty for an offense not previously considered capital[3] as, for instance, the U.S.S.R. decreed the death penalty for stealing from the government. Once the decree has been granted as justified by the needs of society, can anyone within that society believe it ethically wrong, the executions immoral?

Go a step further. Suppose a government decided on the death penalty for people whose continued existence is found contrary to the welfare of its society, as, say,[4] the Nazi government found six million Jews undesirable. We recoil from that act — but on what basis, short of invoking that obsolete concept, God's law?[5] If we believe society's needs to be man's highest law, what can we say was morally wrong? Every Nazi could maintain, and many did, that since the sovereign government of Germany made the law, his function was to obey it; in fact, that he was morally bound to do so. If we no longer believe that God created man, why is human life sacred?

If the taking of human life cannot be logically condmned,[6] except as law condemns it, what of lesser crimes[7]: fraud, embezzlement, rape, adultery, sexual perversion, abortion? Under our new code, can any act whatever[8] —

---

1) without~past : 과거에 뿌리를 박고 있다는 확실한 근거가 없는.
2) Suppose ~ : ~라고 가정해 보자.
3) an offense~capital : 전에는 사형을 내릴 정도라고 생각되지 않았던 죄.
4) as, say, ~ : 예를 들어 ~와 같은.
5) but~law? : 그 낡았다고 버린, 신의 법칙이라는 개념에 의지하지 않고는, 무슨 근거로 (혐오를 느끼는가)? 즉, 신의 법칙에 따라 판단한다는 뜻.
6) logically condemned : 여기서 논리적이라는 말은, 상대적이고 서로 다른 사회적 규범을 근거로 해서가 아니라 만인 공통의 불변의 대원칙을 근거로 해서 추론해 낼 수 있는 것. 즉, 보편 타당한 원리를 기초로 한 것을 뜻함.
7) what~crimes : 그보다 더 사소한 죄들을 더 말할 여지도 없지 않은가.
8) any act whatever : 그 어떤 행동이건.

no matter how gravely offensive— be logically protested or condemned, except by law? And man-made laws vary. In fact, have not parts of the Western world already repealed or suspended their laws against the last three named crimes[1] simply because tastes and attitudes have changed?

And so man left his father's house to live on his own.[2] But was he mature enough for the adventure? He finds his life-held standards[3] dissolving beneath him. Cynicism plagues him, but he cannot refute it; he rejects pure hedonism as a way of life, but he has no philosophy with which to dispute its claims. And, beyond all this, another trouble bewilders, wounds, frightens and embitters him, in the face of which[4] he is as impotent as toward all the rest: the rebellion of his children against him.

Consider the dilemma of the modern parent in the Western world. If, atypically, he is still in possession of his faith that God knows, watches and punishes, then his child growing up in today's world is being alienated from him. The situation resembles that of American immigrant families a few generations ago; the parents spoke a foreign language; the children rejected it, and spoke English. The child cannot help seeing what others are doing, in the secular society, and he cannot help but absorb its outlook and values. Parochial school, bar mitzvah, the threat of Hell, personal example[5] — these may delay the secularization, but cannot prevent it.

Meanwhile, the non-religious parent, or one content merely to observe the forms of a faith,[6] has literally no way to influence his child. He recognizes the utter vacuity of no belief at all[7]; yet he can hardly hold up as a model the

---

1) the last three named crimes : (위의 열거한 것 중)끝으로 세 범죄. 즉 adultery, sexual perversion, abortion.
2) on his own : 자기 혼자 힘으로.
3) life-held standards : 평생 지켜온 기준들.
4) which : 앞의 another trouble을 받음.
5) personal example : 개인적인 수범.
6) one~faith : 신앙의 형식만을 지키는 데에 만족하는 아버지나 어머니.
7) recognizes~all : 신심이 전혀 없으면 철저한 허무가 결과함을 안다.

peculiar lameduck proposition his own life has become: one foot in materialism and one in old-fashioned morality. How can he teach a child to do right if he cannot justify the right?

This parent is in an even worse situation trying[1] to answer the first question that religion used to answer: What is the meaning of man's existence? If a parent must tell a youngster that his life has no meaning, how can he tell him that he should not take drugs? In fact, how can he convince him that he should not commit suicide outright? If the youth does stay alive, it is because he wants to for reasons solely within himself.

Pursue a discussion with any rebellious youth as to why he commits acts that the older generation regards as depraved, self-destuctive or irresponsible, and again and again you will hear the reply, "Why not?" Try to answer "Why not?" If you are a transitional creature[2] living in a half-way house,[3] one who has given up faith while continuing (in order to hold your life together) to act as if you still had it, you have no answer. True, you still — by and large[4] — live by certain moral principles, but you cannot say why. Therein lies the basis of the curious guilt so often felt by parents in the face of[5] insufferable behavior by their young,[6] and their consequent indulgence of children who reject them.

The young rebel's "Why not?" has at least two meanings : not only "What's to stop me?" but simultaneously, "Give me a reason I can accept." For the young person wants, needs, is in fact *desperate* to believe in something. He is in constant search of it — in "mind-bending"[7] drugs, in Zen Buddhism, in

---

1) trying ~ = when he tries ~.
2) a transitional creature : 어중간한 사람. 즉, 종교인도 무종교인도 아닌 사람을 뜻함.
3) a half-way house : 중간에 있는 집. 즉, 어느 쪽인지 분명치 않은 정신적 거주지를 뜻함.
4) by and large : 대체로.
5) in the face of ~ : ~을 당했을 때에.
6) by their young : 앞의 behavior를 수식함.
7) mind-bending : (slang) strongly influencing the mind.

love, astrology, the Peace Corps, a new society, radicalism, hedonism, nihilism, anything but his parents' ism,[1] which he regards as dishonest and cowardly.

The young rebel has not found his belief yet. The experience of learning that an entire civilization is founded on nothing solid morally[2]; that it is shot through and through with[3] what he regards as hypocrisy; that he finds nothing in it to give his life meaning[4] — this has been so overwhelming a shock that it has left him largely mute, inarticulate, confused, unable to cope. He can literally be sure of nothing. And if there is one word that most aptly describes the emotional reaction of the young to finding[5] society without a usable moral basis, it is disgust.

There are still other consequences of man's portentous leap into materialism. In freeing himself of the terror of Hell, he gave up his hope of Heaven : you live, you die, that's the end of it. Your grandfather had the tremendous expectation of a life everlasting. You, typically ambivalent,[6] still hope that somehow it may turn out to be true after all; but your children are, in the most direct sense,[7] hopeless, except for what they can get out of life materialistically.

Further : If man is his own moral judge, and governments derive their powers "from the consent of the governed," then there exists no effective authority. Behind you and me there is only the government we have created; behind the government only the nightstick and the gun. Children are born to parents not as part of a divine plan, but by biological accident. Does that accident confer any authority on the parents? The teacher knows

---

1) parents' ism : 부모가 믿는 것.
2) nothing solid morally : anything that is not morally solid.
3) is shot through and through with ~ : ~으로 가득찼다.
4) to give~meaning : 앞의 nothing을 수식함.
5) to finding ~ : 위의 reaction에 걸림.
6) typically ambivalent = being typically ambivalent.
7) in the most direct sense : 가장 확실한 의미에서.

more facts than the pupil — does that make him an authority? The police, far from personifying authority, are called pigs.[1] The young sneer at Presidents, manhandle deans, burn the nation's flag and display that of its enemy. Why not, if there is no authority?

The idea that man is morally responsible only to himself has been behind the creation of whole new societies : communist, fascist, socialist and shades between[2] — while the older societies are being shaken, changing in nature even as they retain the old names and forms. In the new societies, a kind of morality has been built around protection of the state in what seem like perpetual emergency conditions.[3] But that cannot last; already hippies are plaguing the authorities in Leningrad, Moscow and Prague, and from behind the various curtains[4] we hear protests against the meaninglessness of life.

Meanwhile, Western man finds it increasingly difficult to create for himself a spiritually satisfying life. The traditional religious institutions offer little. Houses of worship have become basketball courts and bingo parlors and places in which to seve a wedding dinner. Already the churchmen, startled by their immense distance from the realities of today's life, have begun to mount the barricades of social protest[5]: you ordain a preceptor of right and wrong, and you get a jazz impresario or a street demonstrator.[6]

Perhaps inevitably, when man no longer needs to beg God for enough food and protection from the elements,[7] he stops begging God. As their

---

1) pigs : 미국에서는 순경을 비하하여 부를 때에 pig라고 함.
2) shades between : 그것들 사이의 약간씩 다른 것들.
3) the state~conditions : 언제나 비상 사태에 처해 있는 것같은 국가.
4) the various curtains : the iron curtain, the bamloo curtains등을 뜻함.
5) mount~protest : 사회적 저항의 바리케이트를 쌓아 올리다. 즉, 사회적 저항에 참여한다는 뜻.
6) you~demonstrator : 옳고 그름을 가려 주는 교시자로 성직자를 서품해 놓으면 그 사람은 재즈 음악회의 주최자가 되거나 가두 시위자가 된다.
7) protection from the elements : 험난한 자연의 힘으로부터 보호.

material needs become satisfied, all people seem headed for the stage[1] in which Western society now finds itself.

And yet the questions remain. Anyone who can contemplate the eye of a housefly, the mechanics of human finger movement, the camouflage of a moth, or the building of every kind of matter from variations in arrangement of proton and electron,[2] and then maintain that all this design happened without a designer, happended by sheer, blind accident — such a person believes in a miracle far more astounding than any in Bible. To regard man, with his arts and aspirations, his awareness of himself and of his universe, his emotions and his morals, his very ability to conceive an idea so grand as that of God, to regard this creature as merely a form of life[3] somewhat higher on the evolutionary ladder than the others, is to create questions more profound than those answered.[4]

Is there no more use for the astonishingly complex human brain than to assure continued existence of the species? Can we not see in the capabilities of the brain some function greater than mere self-preservation? If *all* species seek to preserve themselves, what mindless chemistry created that prodigious urge?[5] If the universe is finite, what exists beyond it? What existed before it began? If it is eternal and limitless, is it not thereby beyond our power ever to know, leaving key questions forever unanswered?

Schoolboy questions, granted[6]; but they will not down.[7] Our materialism

---

1) seem headed for the stage ～ : ～ 단계로 옮아 가는 것 같다.
2) the building～electron : 양자와 전자의 배열이 다르기 때문에 모든 다른 물질이 생긴다는 사실.
3) as merely a form of life : 위의 To regard man과 다음의 to regard this creature에 함께 연결됨. 물론 this creature는 man을 받는다.
4) to create ～answered : (그런 견해가 주는) 해답보다도 더 의미심장한 의문을 야기시키는 것이 된다.
5) what～urge? : 그런 거대한 욕구를 창조해 낸 것은 어떤 무심한 화학작용일까? 즉, 무심한 화학작용일 수 없다는 뜻.
6) Schoolboy questions, granted : 어린 학생의 질문 같다고 하면 그렇다고 인정하겠다.
7) they will not down : 그런 질문들은 결코 수그러들지 않을 것이다.

is itself so shallow, based on blatant assumption that are hardly more than guesswork; impalatable and unsatisfying; demeaning; flagrantly incomplete and yet arrogant in its premises. The idea of God deserves a better substitute.

5. Nature and the Case of Birth Control

By *Robert Ardrey*

In 1932 the director of the New York Aquarium, C.M. Breder, Jr., performed an experiment with guppies that few people are aware of today.[1] Yet the 51 guppies who participated in Breder's adventure should be memorialized, for they have threatened with ruin a scientific doctrine as unquestioned as any in our time.[2]

Guppies multiply lavishly and are born in a ratio of two females for every male. Breder arranged two tanks of equal size, each with food supply and aeration ample to tolerate a host of fish. Then in one tank he placed 50 guppies with an unnatural distribution[3] of approximately one third males, one third females and the remainder juveniles. In the other tank he placed a single female — one heavy with eggs already fetilized. What happened defied explanation.[4]

A remarkable character of the pregnant female guppy is that a single fertilization may give as many as five broods, born every 28 days.[5] The lone female cooperated nobly with the experiment, producing broods as high as 25.[6]

---

1) that ~today : that 이하는 guppies가 아니라 experiment를 수식함.
2) a scientific~time : 우리 시대의 가장 확실한 과학적 원리.
3) an unnatural distribution : 비정상적인 분포.
4) What happened defied explanation : 그 결과 설명하기 어려운 일이 일어났다.
5) that a ~days : 한번 수정하면 28일 만큼씩 다섯배를 낳는다는 것이다.
6) producing ~as 25 : 새끼를 25배나 낳으면서.

Yet at the end of six months there remined only nine fish in her tank. She had eaten the surplus young. In the meantime, the tank with an original population of 50 had witnessed[1] a rapid and immediate die-off. No newborn survived. Cannibalism of the young[2] was so active that it was seldom witnessed.[3] The surviving fish were all from the original population.[4] Here too there were nine. And in both tanks there were three males and six females, the ordained proportion among guppies.

The doctrine the guppies challenged was one that Thomas Malthus, an English economist, had advanced in 1798 in his *Essay on Population*. Malthus demonstrated that while human populations multiply at geometric pace,[5] food supply can increase only by addition.[6] The number of the population must there — fore increase until at some point it overtakes the supply of food. Then, according to Malthus, the population will reach its limits.

The Malthsian logic seemed inarguable,[7] his doctrine a natural law[8] that must apply to all animal species. And yet out of the revolution that has so recently overtaken biology, no proposition is more demonstrable than that a species' population is controlled by the natural self-regulation[9] of numbers — and not by the availability of food. As Breder's guppies demonstrated, rare is the animal population,[10] that has ever expanded until it reached the limits of its food supply. An infinite variety of self-regulatory mechanisms, physiological and behavioral, provide that animal numbers — except in the

1) witnessed = showed.
2) Cannibalism of the young : 새끼를 잡아 먹는 짓.
3) witnessed = observed.
4) the original population : 본래서부터 있던 고기들.
5) at geometric pace : 기하급수적 속도로.
6) by addition : 가산적으로. 즉, 산술급수적으로.
7) inarguable : 반박의 여지가 없는.
8) his doctrine a natural law = his doctrine seems to be a natural law.
9) the natural self-regulation : 자연적인 자기규제.
10) rare is the animal population~ : 도치된 문장. 즉 동물의 수가 ~ 되는 경우는 드물다.

case of climatic catastrophe — will never challenge the carrying capacity[1] of the environment.

By one means or another — reduction of litter size,[2] spontaneous abortion, parental neglect, genetic deterioration, even death by stress — breeding populations[3] are limited. And as the law governs animal groups, it governs primitive human societies as well.

Among all the devices limiting a population, the necessity for a breeding territory is among the most common. Under this system, the female is attracted only by a male who possesses territory of his own. All the other males constitute a non-breeding reserve.[4] This was first thoroughly demonstrated in 1920 by Eliot Howard's observation of countless species of finches and buntings, warblers, lapwings and woodpeckers in which the female is sexually unresponsive to an unpropertied male.[5] Later the same pattern was observed in the Uganda kob, a species of African antelope in which males occupy an arena of territorial competition and to which females are attracted for copulation. Females will accept no other than the successful males.

In many species, of course, the territorial compulsion[6] is absent or fails sufficiently in itself to reduce breeding. Then, neglect of offspring may come into play.[7] For example, the lion, with a relatively short gestation period, preyed on by none,[8] not very susceptible to disease of parasites, could in a few generations be a victim of overpopulation. Yet on Tanzania's great Serengeti Plain, the population of about 1000 lions varies little from season

1) the carrying capacity : 부양능력. 적재량.
2) litter size : 한배에 낳는 새끼 수.
3) breeding populations : 번식할 수 있는 동물의 수.
4) constitute a non-breeding reserve : 번식 못하는 제외자군을 이룬다.
5) an unpropertied male : 영토를 갖지 못한 수컷.
6) the territorial compulsion : 영토를 가지려 하는 강박적인 욕망.
7) come into play : 작용하게 된다.
8) preyed on by none : 아무 것에도 잡아 먹히지 않는.

to season. What keeps their numbers down? Principally maternal neglect, most evident in the lions' order of feeding[1] — males first, females second and cubs last. This compels no great deprivation[2] so long as large game is available. But through the dry season, when food is short, adult appetite is seldom sated, and cubs go hungry. Infant mortality runs to about 50 percent.

The great majority of animal species thus succeed in maintaining relatively stable populations. But there are those that fail and, to keep numbers in order, must suffer the more drastic solution of cyclical population crashes.[3] With a prayerful thought for our own species,[4] let us consider just what happens to them.

The morbid activities of the lemming have been tantalizing the human imagination for centuries. About every three to five years,[5] under the sway of some mysterious compulsion[6] quite unrelated to food supply, the species commits mass suicide, migrating toward water and death by drowning. Investigation of the mystery shifted as early as the 1930s to North America's snowshoe hare,[7] a similar victim of a ten-year cycle. In Minnesota's Lake Alexandria area, zoologists examined numerous corpses. None showed undernourishment, few any evidence of infectious disease. Their manner of death, however, was odd. Some might be behaving normally, others might be in torpor, when suddenly[8] they would be seized by convulsions and die.

---

1) the lions' order of feeding : 사자들의 먹는 순서.
2) This~deprivation : 이것 (어미가 새끼의 먹이를 챙겨주지 않는 것) 때문에 새끼가 크게 줄지 않는다.
3) cyclical population crashes : 주기적인 수의 격감.
4) With~species : 우리 인류를 위해 (이런 일은 없게 해 달라는) 기원하는 마음으로.
5) About every three to five years : 약 매 3~5년마다.
6) under~compulsion : 알 수 없는 어떤 욕망에 휩쓸려서.
7) Investigation~hare : 그 신비에 대한 조사가 일찍이 1930년대에 북미주의 눈신토끼에 대한 조사로 옮겨졌다.
8) when suddenly ~ : 그러다가 갑자기~.

Autopsy showed a certain degenertion in the liver, a deficiency of blood sugar[1] and minor internal hemorrhages.

Most investigators now see such mass deaths as the consequences of social stress in high-density populations. The increasing number of young, the increasing competition of adults, the increasing number of strangers in a massive, increasingly disorganized population at last brings both psychological and physiological exhaustion.

A menace of another order[2] that may come about[3] in rapidly expanding populations is the weakening of the entire gene pool.[4] In an illuminating study, French zoologist François Bourlière records the U.S. government build- up of a herd of reindeer as food supply for the local inhabitants of St. Paul, one of the Pribilof Islands. Here there were no predators at all to weed out the sick, the malformed, the deficient, and for many years the experiment, which began in 1911, seemed a huge success. Four bucks and 21 does were placed on the island and by 1932 they had increased in number to 523, by 1938 to well over 2000. Then came a cataclysmic decline. By 1950 eight remained. The only possible conclusion is that failure by any agency to remove the weak and the deficient from the breeding population gradually sapped the vitality of the whole gene pool. It is a fate many scietists have predicted for the human species.

Thus, throughout all animal species, self-regulatory mechanisms provide that population numbers will never challenge the normal carrying capacity of the physical environment. This principle applies with equal force[5] to primitive peoples, as Sir Alexander Carr-Saunders pointed out almost half a century ago. Within every tribe, he concluded, there is an "optimum

1) blood sugar : 혈당(血糖).
2) of another order : 또 다른 종류의.
3) come about : 일어나다. 발생하다.
4) gene pool = the whole body of genes in an interbreeding population.
5) with equal force : 마찬가지로. 어김없이.

number" about which population fluctuates only slightly.[1] It is a number well under any threat by starvation[2]; yet sufficient to gain a maximum yield from its environment. The number is sustained by varying traditions[3] — by infanticide or compulsory abortion, by cannibalism, head-hunting, human sacrifice, ritual murder, by taboos against incest or against intercourse during the period of lactation.

In modern times, the cultural triumph of humanism — with its respect for the dignity of the indibvidual — has brought the breakdown of such tribal customs. Throughtout a large world of primitive societies,[4] missionaries and colonial masters reacted with horror to such institutions. Tribal warfare was ended. Infanticide was discouraged.

Then the advent of modern medicine and biochemistry struck also at[5] the advanced countries. The rate of infant mortality dropped. Children defective physically or mentally were saved. Human quality was sacrificed for human quantity.

We shall find out one day if, as many biologists fear, overprotection of the human being, like underpredation[6] in the reindeer herd on St. Paul Island, will produce a genetic collapse in the most compassionate populations.[7] If so, it will be an appropriate biological conclusion to a valuable if misdirected philosophy.[8] Yet I find it too neat and simple a conclusion.

Let us review the other possibilities. Human numbers will probably never

---

1) about~slightly : 숫자가 거기서 상하로 약간 넘나들 뿐이다.
2) well~starvation : (인구가 많아) 굶어 죽을 위험한 수치에는 훨씬 못 미치는.
3) varying traditions : 여러 가지 관습.
4) Throughout~societies : 원시 사회로 이루어진 광대한 지역의 어느 곳에서나.
5) struck also at ~ : 또한 ~을 공격했다. 즉 ~ 에 인구 폭발의 공세를 가했다.
6) underpredation : 적절히 잡혀 먹히지 않은 것.
7) the most compassionate populations : 가장 인도적인 (즉 심신 장애자들을 자연도태시키지 않고 모두 살려 내는) 부류의 사람들.
8) an appropriate~philosophy : 혹시 빗나간 것인지는 모르나 가치 있는 철학 (즉 인도주의)에 대한 적절한 생리학적 결론.

reach such magnitude as to encounter the limitations of food supply. Long before such a rendezvous[1] can take place, other forces will have affected our numbers. If we take nature as a model, there are two probabilities. The first is a sane and humane program of population control, as a cultural substitute for innate behavioral patterns.[2] The second is death by stress.

Population control, whatever form it takes, must be mandatory to be successful. We must consider enforced contraception,[3] whether through taxation on surplus children, or through more severe means such as conception license, replacing or supplementing marriage license. Abortion should be freely available to those suffering unintended pregnancy.[4] In international relation, of course, any aid to peoples who through ignornace, prejudice or political hypnosis fail to control their numbers might be forbidden. Such a program sounds more formidable than it would probably prove to be,[5] for any institution which accords with the laws of nature rarely fails.

Birth control, a solution both sane and humane, has, of course, its alternative. But the alternative, death by stress, is a messy one indeed. For example, if we accept an insane solution as preferable to a sane one, then we must see that the automobile is an excellent instrument for reducing the breeding population. With its rising accident rate, it stikes most heavily at the young, in numbers mathematically determined by population density.[6]

If life in the megalopolis discourages large families, then perhaps by discriminatory taxation[7] falling most heavily on real estate we might

---

1) such a rendezvous : 인구증가가 식량조달의 한계와 만나는 것을 뜻함.
2) a cultural~patterns : (원시인이나 동물에서 볼 수 있는) 선천적 행동양식 대신에 문화적(후천적)인 대치물.
3) enforced contraception : 강제적인 피임.
4) those suffering unintended pregnancy : 원하지 않는 임신을 당하는 사람들.
5) than~be : 실제보다.
6) in numbers ~ density : 인구밀도에 의해 수학적으로 결정되는 수 만큼.
7) discriminatory taxation : 차등과세.

reverse the flight to the suburbs and drive middle-class families back to the unpleasantness of urban reproduction.[1] We should have nothing to lose by such a move, in any case, since further concentrations of city life must produce more stress, more broken marriages, more impotency due to acute alcoholism, more corpses, victims of crime in the streets and more couples living together in unreproductive sin.[2]

War, too, could be useful. But wars today simply do not kill enough people. A nuclear conflict could of course leave us with no population problem at all. But even as highly publicized a war as that in Vietnam has failed throughout its entire course to kill as many Americans as the automobile kills in a normal year.

We must look to more imaginative agencies.[3] I am sure, for example, that when our population has again doubled, when not a water supply remains unpolluted, when the traffic jams of tomorrow make today's seem memories of the open road, when civil disorder has permanently replaced war[4] as a form of organized violence, when the air of the city can no longer be breathed and the countryside has vanished, when crime has become so prevalent that no citizen goes unarmed, when varieties of[5] rage and frustration remain the only emotions man or woman can know, then perhaps we shall comprehend the lemming.

But of course future times of such stressful wonder may never come to be.[6] Somewhere along the road[7] we may choose compulsory contraception. And yet no one can make a sure prediction. *Homo sapiens*, that creature mad

1) the unpleasantness of urban reproduction : 도시에서 아이를 낳아 기르는 불유쾌함.
2) unreproductive sin : 비생식적인 죄악. 즉 비정상적인 성행위를 뜻함.
3) look ~ agencies : 보다 더 신기한 방법에 기대를 걸다.
4) replace war : 전쟁을 대체하다. 즉 전쟁을 능가한다는 뜻.
5) varieties of : 여러 가지.
6) may never come to be : 오지 않을는지 모른다.
7) Somewhere along the road : 그러는 과정 어디쯤에선가.

beyond the craziest of hares,[1] lunatic beyond all lemmings, may go to the end of the road with no impulse more logical than to discover what lies there.[2] Our tragedy and our magnificence together rise from the same smoky truth[3] that we alone among animal species refuse to acknowledge natural law.

---

1) the craziest of hares : cf. mad as a (March) hare. 토끼는 미친 것 같이 행동하는 경우가 많음.

2) with～there : 마지막에 무엇이 있는지 알아 보자는 것보다 더 논리적인 충동이 없이. 즉 마지막까지 가 보자는 비논리적인 충동만으로.

3) smoky truth : 연기에 쌓인 진실. 즉 정체가 무엇인지 잘 알 수 없는 진실이라는 뜻.

6. Four Choices for Young People

By *Penny Porter*

Shortly before his graduation, Jim Binns, president of the senior class at Stanford University, wrote me about some of his misgivings. "More than any other generation," he said, "our generation views the adult world with great skepticism...there is also an increased tendency to[1] reject completely that world."

Apparently he speaks for[2] a lot of his contemporaries. During the last few years, I have listened to scores of[3] young people, in college and out,[4] who were just as nervous about[5] the grown-up world. Roughly, their attitude might be summed up about like this:[6] "The world is in pretty much of a mess,[7] full of injustice, poverty, and war. The people responsible are, presumably, the adults who have been running things.[8] If they can't do better than that, what have they got to teach our generation?[9] That kind of lesson we can do without."[10]

---

1) there~to ~ : ~하는 경향 또한 더 커져 있다.
2) speak for ~ : ~을 대변하다.
3) scores of : 수 많은. score는 20을 뜻함.
4) in college and out : out는 out of college의 뜻. 이 구는 앞의 young people에 걸리는 형용사구임.
5) who~about ~ : ~에 대해 (그와) 꼭 마찬가지로 걱정하는.
6) about like this : 대략 다음과 같이.
7) is in pretty much of mess : 상당히 엉망인 상태에 있다.
8) who~things : 세상의 일들을 주관해 온.
9) to teach our generation : What를 수식하는 형용사구.
10) do without : 없이 지내다. That kind of lesson이 without 의 목적어임.

These conclusions strike me as reasonable,[1] at least from their point of view. The relevant question for the arriving generation is not whether our society is imperfect (we can take that for granted), but how to deal with it. For all[2] its harshness and irrationality, it is the only world we've got. Choosing a strategy to cope with it,[3] then, is the first decision young adults have to make, and usually the most important decision of their lifetime. So far as I have been able to discover, there are only four basic alternatives:

1. Drop Out[4]

This is one of the oldest expedients, and it can be practiced anywhere, at any age, and with or without the use of hallucinogens. It always has been the strategy of choice for people[5] who find the world too brutal or too complex to be endured. By definition,[6] this way of life is parasitic. In one way or another, its practitioners batten on[7] the society which they scorn and in which they refuse to take any responsibility. Some of us find this distasteful — an undignified kind of life.[8] But for the poor in spirit,[9] with low levels of both energy and pride, it may be the least intolerable choice available.

2. Flee

This strategy also has ancient antecedents. Ever since civilization began, certain individuals have tried to run away from it in hopes of finding a

1) strike me as reasonable : 내게는 타당하게 느껴진다.
2) For all ~ : ~에도 불구하고.
3) cope with it : 그것을 잘 처리하다.
4) drop out : 탈락하다. 이탈하다.
5) the strategy of choice for people ~ : ~한 사람들이 선택하는 전략.
6) By definition : 정의하면. 그 말 자체가 의미하듯이.
7) batten on ~ : ~을 잔뜩 먹다. ~을 이용하여 잘 먹다.
8) an undignified ~life : this 의 보어.
9) the poor in spirit : 기백이 약한 자들.

simpler, more pastoral, and more peaceful life. Unlike the dropouts, they are not parasites. They are willing to support themselves[1] and to contribute something to the general community, but they simply don't like the environment of civilization; that is, the city,[2] with all[3] its ugliness and tension.

The trouble with this solution is that it no longer is practical on a large scale. Our planet, unfortunately, is running out of noble savages[4] and unsullied landscapes; except for the polar regions, the frontiers are gone. A few gentleman farmers[5] with plenty of money can still escape to the bucolic life — but in general the stream of migration is flowing the other way.[6]

3. Plot a Revolution

This strategy is always popular among those who have no patience with[7] the tedious workings of the democratic process or who believe that basic institutions can only be changed by force. It attracts some of the more active and idealistic young people of every generation. To them it offers a romantic appeal, usually symbolized by some dashing and charismatic figure. It has the even greater appeal of simplicity.[8] "Since this society is hopelessly bad, let's smash it and build something better on the ruins."[9]

Some of my best friends have been revolutionists, and a few of them have led resonably satisfying lives. These[10] are the ones whose revolutions did

---

1) support themselves : 자기 앞은 자기가 가리다.
2) the city : 앞의 the environment of civilization과 동격.
3) with all ~ : 모든 ~ 것들을 가진. 여기서 with all~ 는 ~에도 불구하고의 뜻이 아님.
4) noble savages : 숭고한 야만인. 서양서 18, 19세기에 유행한 말로서 문명에 물들지 않고, 자연적인 덕성을 지닌 미개인을 뜻함.
5) gentleman farmers : 취미로 농사 짓는 사람들.
6) the other way : 그 반대 방향으로.
7) have no patience with ~ : ~을 참지 못하다.
8) even~simplicity : 간명성이라는 좀 더 큰 호소력.
9) on the ruins : 그 폐허 위에.
10) These : a few of them 을 받음. 즉 상당히 만족한 삶을 산 자들.

not come off[1]; they have been able to keep on cheerfully ploting their holocausts right into their senescence.[2] Others died young, in prison or on the barricades.[3] But the most unfortunate are those whose revolutions have succeeded. They lived, in bitter disillusionment, to see[4] the establishment they had over-thrown replaced by[5] a new one, just as hard-faced and stuffy.[6]

I am not, of course, suggesting that revolutions accomplish nothing. Some (the American Revolution, the French Revolution) clearly do change things for the better.[7] My point is merely that the idealists who make the rvolution are bound to be disappointed in either case. For at best[8] their victory never dawns on the shining new world[9] they had dreamed of, cleansed of all human meanness.[10] Instead it dawns on a familiar, workaday place, still in need of groceries and sewage disposal.[11] The revolutionary state, under whatever political label, has to be run — not by violent romantics — but by experts in marketing, sanitary engineering,[12] and the management of bureaucracies.

---

1) come off : 성공하다. 실현되다.
2) right into their senescence : 노년에까지 계속. right는 강조의 뜻.
3) on the barricades : 싸우다가.
4) to see : 결과적으로 해석할 것.
5) replaced by : the establishment의 보어.
6) just~stuffy : a new one을 수식하는 형용사구.
7) for the better : 좋은 방향으로.
8) at best : 아무리 좋아도.
9) their victory ~world : 승리의 새 날이 빛나는 새 세상 위에 밝아 오는 법은 없다.
10) cleansed ~meanness : the shining new world를 수식하는 형용사구.
11) still~disposal : a familiar, workaday place를 수식하는 형용사구.
12) sanitary engineering : 위생공학 (상.하수도, 냉.난방 등).

4. Try To Change the World Gradually, One Clod at a Time

At first glance, this course is far from inviting.[1] It lacks glamour. It promises no quick results. It depends on the exasperating and uncertain instruments of persuasion and democratic decision making. It demands patience, always in short supply.[2] About all that can be said for it is[3] that it sometimes works — that in this particular time and place it offers a better chance for remedying some of the world's outrages than any other available strategy.

So[4] at least the historical evidence seems to suggest. When I was graduating from college, my generation also found the world in a mess.[5] The economic machinery[6] had broken down almost everywhere: in this country nearly a quarter of the population was out of work. A major war seemed all too likely.[7] As a college newspaper editor at that time, I protested against this just as vehemently as student activists are protesting today.

At the same time, my generation was discovering that reforming the world is a little like fighting a military campaign in the Apennines;[8] as soon as you capture one mountain range, another one looms just ahead. As the big problems of the thirties were brought under some kind of rough control,[9] new problems took their place — the unprecedented problems of an affluent society, of racial justice, of keeping our cities from becoming uninhabitable, of coping with war in unfamiliar guises.[10] Most disturbing of all was our

---

1) far from inviting : 전혀 매력이 없는.
2) always in short supply : 항상 부족한. patience에 걸림.
3) About~is ~ : 그것을 지지해 말할 수 있는 것은 ~이 고작이다.
4) So : 그렇다고.
5) in a mess : 엉망 상태인.
6) economic machinery : 경제 구조.
7) seemed all too likely : 일어날 가능성이 대단히 커 보였다.
8) fighting~Apennines : 아페닌 산맥에서 군사작전을 수행하는 것.
9) were~control : 어떻게 해서 대강 해결이 되었다.
10) war in unfamiliar guises : 옛날과는 다른, 여러 가지로 위장된 전쟁.

discovery of[1] the population explosion. It dawned on us[2] rather suddenly that the number of passengers on the small spaceship[3] we inhabit is doubling about every forty years. So long as the earth's population keeps growing at this cancerous rate, all of the other problems appear virtually insoluble. Our cities will continue to become more crowded and noisome. The landscape will get more cluttered, the air and water even dirtier. The quality of life is likely to become steadily worse for everybody. And warfare on a rising scale[4] seems inevitable if too many bodies have to struggle for ever — dwindling share of food and living space.

So Jim Binns' generation has a formidable job on its hands.[5] But not, I think, an insuperable one.[6] On the evidence of the past,[7] it can be handled in the same way that hard problems have been coped with before — piecemeal, pragmatically by the dogged efforts of many people.

---

1) was our discovery of ~ : 주어와 동사가 도치되었음.
2) dawned on us : 우리에게 어렴풋이 의식되었다.
3) the small spaceship : 지구를 비유하는 말임.
4) at this cancerous rate : 이런 암과 같이 빠른 속도로.
5) warfare on a rising scale : 규모가 점점 커져 가는 전쟁.
6) on its hands : 그들의 책임 (또는 부담)이 되어.
7) But not~one = but it is not, I think, an insuperable one (job).
8) On~past : 과거의 증거를 미루어 생각하면.

7. I Became a Bum

By *Steve Bacon*

If I hadn't been hungry, broke and exhausted to the point of blindness[1) I would have walked out, but under the circumstances my slum hotel accommodations were more than welcome. Opening a door off[2) a small, dank corridor, the innkeeper issued me into a black, windowless cubicle measuring eight by 10 feet and fumbled for a light chain.[3) The bare bulb came on[4) to reveal[5) dirty, vomit-stained pink walls, a dripping sink in one corner, a disreputable-looking bed and a dresser with one drawer.

"How about the key?" [6) I mumbled, dropping my canvas bag on the floor. "Naw, You lock yourself in."[7) the man replied anxious to get back to the TV in the front room that doubled as an office[8) : "If you go out, nobody will bother your stuff." I hadn't had much sleep in the last 30 hours, and it took too much effort to follow his logic. After quickly deciding to ignore the roaches, the steady dripping from the sink and the moaning of an addict

---

1) to the point of blindness : 눈이 안 보일 정도로.
2) off = from.
3) light chain : 전등의 스위치에 연결된 줄.
4) came on : 작동됐다. 즉 불이 들어왔다.
5) to reveal : 결과적으로 해석할 것.
6) How about the key ? : 열쇠는 어떻게 된 거요? 즉 열쇠는 안 주느냐는 뜻.
7) You lock yourself in : (열쇠를 주었다가는) 안에서 잘못해 문을 잠가버려 못나오게 된다.
8) that doubled as an office : 사무실로 겸용되고 있는.

suffering withdrawal symptoms[1] in the next room, I lay down on the bed and slept.

A burglar would have had slim pickings.[2] My entire fortune consisted of $ 1.16 in change and a battered bag containing one set of underwear and a pair of socks. I was without wallet or identification. Nothing linked me to middle-class respectability except a well-folded letter in my shirt pocket that I was pledged to use only in dire emergency. The letter, from an official agency of the State of New Jersey, identified me as a participant in one of the hardest-hitting societal sensitivity programs[3] ever devised: the Immersion Program sponsored by the Trenton, N.J.-based[4] Department of Community Affairs. The goal of the Immersion Program[5] (and similar training programs in other parts of the country) is to give administrators, educators, businessmen and other professionals the smell, taste and feel of poverty as it[6] really exists . After living in it, they become sensitized to its victims, and begin to understand the faults of agencies set up to help the poor. To the extent that it is possible to do so in 48 hours,[7] immersion provides a direct, personal poverty experience — and leaves the shaken participants with some idea of the daily battle for survival that must be waged by a large segment of the population.

New Jersey's "school of hard knocks"[8] was started in the fall of 1968, inspired by a similar program set up in Baltimore for administrative

---

1) withdrawal symptons : (마약 중독의) 금단 증상 (욕지기, 발한, 허탈 등).
2) would~pickings : 도둑질해 갈 만한 것이 별로 없었을 것이다.
3) the hardest-hitting ~program : 가장 강력한 사회 감응 계획.
4) the Trenton, N.J.-based : 뉴저지주 트렌튼에 기지를 둔.
5) the Immersion Program : 잠입 체험 계획.
6) it : the smell, taste and feel of poverty를 받음. smell, taste, feel을 각각으로 보지 않은 것은 정관사 the를 앞에 하나만 붙인 것으로 알 수 있음.
7) To the extent~hour : 48시간 내에 가능한 최대한도로.
8) knock = a blow or misfortune of hard treatment. 즉, 고생. ex. The school of hard knocks gave him a tenacious grasp of reality.

members of the U.S. Department of Health, Education and Welfare. Even tougher programs are in existence in Chicago, Los Angeles, Atlanta and a number of smaller localities. Pioneer among them is "The plunge" established in Chicago in 1964 by the Urban Training Center for Christian Mission. It sends men and women of the church out into the streets for a week-long exposure to the poverty culture.[1] They are dressed in old clothes and are given an allowance of a dollar a day. There's no place for them to stay when darkness falls.

I volunteered for the New Jersey program just before Christmas, and the letter from Robert C. Holmes, its director, spelled out[2] the details. I was to report to a small, economically-depressed New Jersey town about an hour from New York. I should dress in down-and-out clothing and sport several days growth of beard.[3] I would be permitted a "welfare allowance"[4] of $2 for food and shelter for two days.

Although immersion has to be experienced as a loner, there were eight of us at the orientation session held in a local church basement. Bob Holmes, a 29-year-old educator and veteran of the Peace Corps, briefly described the goals of the program and how to contact various welfare agencies and private organizations for food and shelter once the going got rough.[5] The next job was to develop a cover story[6]: I would be role-playing in talking to these agencies, and I wanted them to accept me for what I appeared to be[7]: a broke, homeless transient.[8] My story was relatively simple. I was posing as a cab driver from Chicago—a city I happen to know well. An old Army

1) a week-long~culture : 빈민 문화를 일 주일 동안 체험하게 하기 위해서.
2) spelld out : 명확히 설명해 주었다.
3) sport~beard : 며칠 자란 턱수염을 깎지 않고 그대로 두다. sport = wear, display.
4) welfare allowance : 복지 급여액.
5) once the going got rough : 일이 어려워지면. 즉, 실제 체험에 들어 갔을 때를 뜻함.
6) develop a cover story : 거짓말 사연을 만들어 내다.
7) to accept~to be : 내 행색이 말해주는 대로 나를 생각해 주기를.
8) transient = a temporary visitor or worker.

buddy who lived in town supposedly had invited me back East and had offered to help me find a good job. Unfortunately, my friend was nowhere to be found when I arrived on that snowy December evening, and I was stranded without food, shelter of bus fare back home.[1]

It all seemed like a lark[2] setting out from the warm church basement about 9:30 without wallet or identification. I headed for the local Salvation Army with $2 in change in my pocket. They'd put me up[3] for one night, I was sure, and I'd find work on Monday morning. The temperature was below freezing as I walked the mile to the mission,[4] but the way was brightened by Christmas lights twinkling overhead. Only after arriving at the dingy, three-story brick building did I lose my false sense of security. It was closed, locked tight and shuttered, and no amount of banging brought[5] the Salvationist Captain to the door.

Well, I've really let myself in for it,[6] I thought, heading back up the thoroughfare through the center of town. The local YMCA was close by, and I thought of asking if they had an inexpensive room or even a cot they could put up in the hallway. A bit self-conscious,[7] I walked into the building and set the bag on the floor in front of the desk while the guy behind it eyed me suspiciously.

"Do you have a room?" I asked.

"Sure," he said turning to the card file. Then he turned back and gave me a good going over[8]: "Nope. I'm wrong. We're all filled up."

---

1) bus fare back home : 집으로 돌아갈 버스비.
2) seemed like a lark : 재미있는 장난 같았다.
3) put me up : 나를 재워주다.
4) the mission : 자선 단체.
5) no~brought ~ : 아무리 두드려도 ~ 이 나타나지 않았다.
6) in for it : 큰 탈이 난.
7) A bit self~conscious : 좀 쭈뼛쭈뼛하면서.
8) going over : 자세히 뜯어 보는것. 철저한 심문(또는 조사).

"Do you know where I can stay for one night?" I persisted. After he advised me to try the Holiday Inn, I told him I didn't have much money.

"Well, there are some hotels and boarding houses down on Front Street," he said disinterestedly. "It's kind of dangerous down there,[1] but that's all there is." As I picked up my bag, he busied himself with shuffling papers, thoroughly relieved not to be[2] further burdened with my problem.

A long walk the length of Front Street[3] where I'd gotten off the bus just a few hours before confirmed my worst fears. There were cheap, shabby hotels, but the least I could get a room for[4] was $5 — some $3 more than I had to live on for the next two days, A thin, gray-haired derelict stood in a doorway, and I asked him if he knew where I could find a bed for the night. After he told me what I had already discovered — that there wasn't an open mission in town — I asked him about the railroad station which was close by.

"I just got chased out." he said. "They have some new detectives over there." He told me about the local police and that I should avoid them if at all possible.[5] Grateful for his advice,[6] I suddenly felt ashamed at the number of times I had ignored others like him who are often in situations even more desperate than mine.

I had no choice now; it would have to be the railroad station, at least until the police or railroad detectives caught up with me.[7] I walked into the dirty, flourescent-lighted waiting room and sat down. A few minutes later, tired from walking in the cold for the last two hours, I was lying down. A sharp rap on the sole of one shoe interrupted my dozing, and it was coupled

1) It's～there : 그곳은 좀 위험하다.
2) thoroughly relieved not to be ～ : ～하지 않게 되어 아주 마음이 홀가분해져서.
3) the length of Front Street : Front Street의 처음에서 끝에 이르는.
4) the least～for : 가장 싼 방값.
5) if at all possible : 거의 불가능하지만.
6) Grateful for his advice = Feeling grateful for his advice.
7) caught up with : 따라와 잡았다.

with an admonition[1] from the cop on the beat[2] to "sit up." A few minutes later a railroad detective I had been warned about got his crack in."[3] Where you going?" he asked. "New York." I replied, trying to be as nonchalant as possible." The last train leaves at 1:00 A.M. You can't spend the night here,"

He moved on, glancing back over his shoulder to make sure I got the message.

I sat up and looked at the clock. It was now 10 minutes to midnight. I had no place to sleep, it was cold outside and to make matters worse,[4] I was feeling the call of nature.[5] The only toilet in the station cost a dime, and I debated whether to spend the 10 cents or to wait and dash in when somebody came out. The matter was decided when an elderly man came out and the door remained slightly ajar.

Finding sleep impossible in an upright position, I hypnotized myself[6] by watching the large clock on the wall, dreading 1:00 A.M. and the necessity of returning to the cold street. Two blacks dressed in broadbrim hats and furcoats caught my attention. They stood talking until a pay phone[7] rang on a prearranged signal.[8] The subject was drugs and, casting an eye around to make sure they were unobserved by the cop who had been there earlier, they sauntered out to do some dealing.[9] A short time later a sad-looking prositute eyed the remnants — down to four including myself[10]— and moved on to better hunting grounds. The clock now read 1:10 and it looked

---

1) it~admonition : 그것 (a sharp rap on the sole)은 곧 경고로 이어졌다.
2) on the beat : 순찰중인.
3) got his crack in : 그의 비아냥거리는 말을 던졌다.
4) to make matters worse : 일을 더 난처하게 만든 것은.
5) the call of nature : 용변.
6) hypnotize myself : 자신에게 최면을 걸었다. 즉 억지로 잠든 상태에 들려고 했다는 뜻.
7) pay phone : (동전을 넣어야 작동되는) 공중전화.
8) on a prearranged signal : 예정된 신호에 따라.
9) dealing : 마약 거래.
10) down~myself : 나를 포함해 네 명으로 줄어 든.

like the law was going to relent,[1] but then the railroad man was there to turn us out.[2]

"Where can I stay?" I protested when he asked me to leave. " I don't have any money." " There's an all-night restaurant over there," he said, pointing across the street. "You can sit over there."

A cup of coffee was the price of my refuge from the cold, and I ordered it, spreading out in a booth[3] and trying to get as comfortable as possible. Pouring plenty of sugar in it, I sipped it slowly to make it last. This game went on for an hour until the Greek restaurant owner began to lose his patience. He growled to the cook, shook his head and slammed a tray on the counter.

"No," I didn't want anything more, I answered to his repeated inquiries. "You stay here all night ?" he finally asked." That isn't nice."

Mumbling something about waiting for a friend, I got up and paid 16 cents for the coffee. I now had $1.84 and three hours to go until daylight.

The streets of the town were deserted as I walked through them, considering the possibility of camping out in a doorway[4] or finding an open entrance to a building where I could at least get out of the cold.[5] No such luck; they were all locked. Should I call home, I wondered? 4:00 A.M. I again tried train station, and the railroad employee took a sort of sadistic pity on me. "O.K.," he grinned. "You come back in, but you stand on your feet until morning." Anything was better than the cold, and I stood next to[6] a steam radiator, letting the warmth sink in.

The first order of business[7] would be a place to stay and then a job, and I

---

1) it~relent : 법(기차를 탈 사람이 아니면 내쫓는)이 온정을 보여 줄 것 같았다.
2) to turn us out : 우리를 내쫓기 위해.
3) spreading out in a booth : 자리에 축 펴지게 앉아서.
4) camping~doorway : 임시로 어느 집 현관에서 밤을 지낼.
5) get out of the cold : 한둔을 면하다. 추위를 피하다.
6) next to ~ : ~에 붙어서.
7) The first order of business : 제일 첫째 할 일.

resolved to get working on that as soon as I could get something to eat. Six o'clock found a greasy spoon[1] opening down the street, and for 68 cents the waitress delivered fried potatoes, two pieces of toast, scrambled eggs and coffee. I felt warm and well fed as I strode out — without leaving a tip — with $1.16 in my pocket.

A little later I staked out[2] the city welfare office and hung around the door waiting for the 9:00 A.M. opening. Poverty was having an effect.[3] I found myself becoming deferential as the arriving workers[4] glanced at me, then quickly looked away. A guard reluctantly directed me to a bathroom and I put my head under the cold water, trying to clear away the cobwebs.[5] When the welfare office opened for business, I found myself telling my story in a quavering voice to a brusque, stout, discourteous woman employee.

Yes, city welfare could offer some help, but I had to have an address within the city[6] "But I need help to find a place to stay" I almost shouted. Yes, it was too bad, but those were the rules. I should come back when I had a place to stay.

After this setback I made a mile trek to a store-front agency,[7] in a predominantly black and Puerto Rican neighborhood. The agency, known as the Multi-Service Center, had been labeled a possibility[8] by Bob Holmes, and it turned out to be a good tip. A sympathetic social worker listened to my story, jotted down a few details, made a phone call and then handed me

---

1) greasy spoon : 싸고 지저분한 식당.
2) staked out ~ : ~을 감시했다. 즉 멀리서 지켜봤다는 뜻.
3) Poverty~effect : 가난이 내게 영향을 끼치고 있었다.
4) workers : (복지 사무소에서) 근무하는 사람들.
5) cobwebs = confusion, indistinctness, of lack of order.
6) Yes, city ~ the city : 이 부분은 위의 woman employee가 한 말을 인칭과 시제만 바꾸어 쓴 것임.
7) make ~ agency : 가게새처럼 길가에 있는 자선단체로 한 마일을 터덜터덜 걸어 갔다.
8) had ~ possibility : 실제적인 도움을 받을 수 있는 곳이라고 분류된.

a slip of paper with an address. Reverend Baker, minister of the local Baptist Church, would help me find a place to stay. His church was a mile and a half away, but it seemed like nothing[1]: I would have a place to rest. Tomorrow I could report to the man-power pool[2] and maybe get a job.

I found Baker's Church and wandered in, hat in hand.[3] He greeted me warmly and a short time later I was installed in the windowless "pink" room on dangerous Front Street. Despite the roaches, the dripping water and the bed that sagged into a back-breaking "U,"[4] I was asleep 10 minutes later.

It was dark outside when I awoke to the thuds of furniture[5] being thrown against the wall by the delirious drug-addict next door. That didn't bother me but I was hungry again, and I put on my coat and sleepily started to cross the street, being narrowly missed by a car[6] which came rushing through. "Too bad he didn't run him over?"[7] I heard a bystander say to the woman next to him. "I wish they'd run the drifters out of town."

Picking myself up,[8] I went into a pizza parlor where 66 cents bought two slices of pizza and a cup of coffee. Fifty cents left and one day to go.[9] I would have to find a job tomorrow if I wanted to eat. The Multi-Service Center had told me to go to the man-power pool and to get there early if I wanted to eat. There was already a line by 7:00 A.M. the next morning.

"You want a job loading trucks?"[10] The heavy, gray-haired counselor asked me when my turn came.

"Sure. But I need money right now to eat. When do they pay?" I asked him.

---

1) it ~ nothing : 그 거리가 아무 것도 아닌 것 같았다.
2) the man ~ power pool : 합동 인력 소개소.
3) hat in hand : 공손한 태도로.
4) a back-breaking "U" : 침대의 가운데가 U자형으로 쳐지면 허리가 아픈 것을 말함.
5) awoke~furniture : 깨어나니 가구 부딪치는 소리가 났다.
6) being~car : 그리고 하마터면 자동차에 치일 뻔 했다.
7) Too bad ~ over : 그를 치어 버리지 않은 것이 유감이군.
8) Picking myself up : 일어나서.
9) Fifty~go : 앞에 I had를 넣어 생각할 것.
10) you~trucks ? : 트럭에 짐 싣는 일을 하겠나?

"You don't get paid till Friday," the man told me, gesturing to a sign on the wall. "We don't give advances." My heart sank, and I stared at him, making him a bit nervous. "Sorry," he said. "Those are the rules."

Thanking him and telling him I'd think about it, I wandered back out into the cold. Thirty cents bought me coffee and a roll, and I decided to try an employment agency. They were no help either, and when I told them there was no place they could call for references,[1] the girl practically pushed me out of the door. I started to buy a paper with one of my last two dimes to look at the help-wanted ads,[2] then thought better of it[3] and headed for the local library.

The paper was no help, and even if anyone had advertised for day labor it was already too late in the day to start. And if I wanted a place to stay tonight, I'd have to go back to Reverend Baker. The roll had been consumed at 7:30 A.M. and it was well past noon. Food was now the problem, but the Salvation Army was still locked, and on a second try,[4] the city welfare would not offer even so much as a meal ticket. I stopped by the Red Cross only to learn they might be able to feed me — if I came back well after lunch hour.

The good smell of food from a Hebrew Day School was the last straw.[5] Abandoning my last iota of pride, I went in, found the rabbi, and asked for food. The generous plate of hamburgers and beans tasted better than anything I have ever eaten.

I had to have money, and the only way left to get it was to panhandle. Cautiously I approached a well-dressed citizen, asking if he could spare a little change. No luck. He walked on by and so did the next five people I

---

1) there~references : 신원보증을 위해서 전화로 알아볼데가 없다고.
2) help-wanted ads : 구인광고란.
3) thought better of it : 고쳐 생각했다.
4) on a second try : 두번째로 가 본 곳에서는.
5) was the last straw : 더 버틸 수 없게 했다.

asked, their eyes turning away from me to the street, a store window or — in a few cases — staring at me with disgust. A sudden inspiration took me down the street to a bus stop. Two women were waiting for the bus. Keeping an eye out for cops,[1] I told them I needed just enough change to get home. It worked. One dug out[2] a dime and the other gave me 15 cents.

Embarrassed to let them see I was panhandling, I waited until they boarded the bus, then tried another tired commuter. He refused and so did the next, but I kept at it for over an hour until I had 65 cents — the hardest money I have ever earned. What stopped me was the waspish[3] little man who screamed, "Get out of here! Get going before I call the police!"

Why do individuals, welfare agencies and other charitable organizations refuse requests for help to find a place to sleep or just to get a square meal? In part, guilt plays a role,[4] for many of those I asked for assistance were apologetic, yet anxious to suppress in their own minds the fact that I was in real trouble. "There are other people or agencies that will help you," was their unspoken comment. "We'd like to, but we can't. Please leave us alone; you make us feel uncomfortable."

Yet another reason for ignoring appeals for help stems from the fear that if a locality proves to be an easy mark[5] the poor will make even greater demands and become more and more dependent upon its scarce resources. "Go back where you came from." says the welfare agency. "We'll help only our own poor."

A tradition that links success with virtue and failure with inherent

1) keeping~cops : 순경들이 있나 조심하면서.
2) dug out : (주머니에서) 찾아내었다.
3) waspish : 심술궂은. 그러나 WASP (White Angle-Saxon Protestant)의 암시도 있음.
4) guilt plays a role : 죄의식이 한 몫을 하고 있다. 즉 죄의식이 한 원인이라는 뜻.
5) if ~ mark : 한 지역을 맡고 있는 자선사업단체의 한 지회가 만만한 봉이라고 생각되면.

weakness — in what is defined as a land of opportunity[1] — aggravates the problem. "We manage to live well enough, why can't you?" is the unspoken accusation. "There is no place for the poor in our society," confirms Bob Holmes. He might also have added that being poor leads to persecution — as witness[2] my night spent between the train station and the streets.

What do others who have participated in the Immersion Program have to say? Dr. Richard Bjork, president of New Jersey's New Richard Stockton State College, says "I encountered hostility, suspicion and indifference from people who had more than I did. They walked by me and would not even answer questions let alone[3] provide food or shelter. The people who had the least were the most willing to help.

"My worst experience was with the Savation Army, and the Rescue Mission. They felt they were doing you a favor; evidently they had become hardened and cynical. When I asked the Salvation Army for a bed for the night, they told me, 'We don't take people like you any more.'

---

1) in what～opportunity : 기회의 나라라고 불리는 곳에서.
2) as witness : 그 증거로는. 이를테면.
3) let alone ～ : ～는 커녕.

PART Ⅱ

*Fenstad's Mother

By *Charles Baxter**

* Fenstad's Mother"는 1988년 The Atlantic 지에 게재된 단편소설로, 기독교도인 주인공과 사회주의자인 어머니, 그리고 주인공의 애인과 야간 대학 학생들의 뒤얽힌 관계를 통해 따뜻한 인간관계를 보여준다. 또한 주인공과 그의 어머니 사이에 보여지는 60년대의 혁신적 사고와 80년대의 보수적 사고의 대립은, 80년대에 점차 보수적으로 되어가는 현대 미국 사회를 형상화하고 있다 : Charles Baxter (1947~)

On Sunday morning after Communion[1] Fenstad drove across town to visit his mother. Behind the wheel,[2] he exhaled with his hand flat in front of his mouth to determine if the wine on his breath could be detected. He didn't think so. Fenstad's mother was a lifelong social progressive[3] who was amused by her son's churchgoing, and, wine or no wine,[4] she could guess where he had been. She had spent her life in the company of rebels and deviationists[5], and[6] she recognized all their styles.

Passing a frozen pond in the city park, Fenstad slowed down to watch the skaters, many of whom he knew by name and skating style. From a distance they were dots of color ready for flight, frictionless.[7] To express grief on skates seemed almost

1) Communion = Holy Communion
2) Behind the wheel : 운전석에 앉아서, 운전을 하면서.
3) a lifelong social progressive : 강경한 진보적 사회주의자.
4) wine or no wine : 술을 마셨건 안 마셨건.
5) rebels and deviationists : (당노선으로부터의)반항자들과 이탈자들.
6) ,and : 그래서.
7) frictionless : 마찰이 없는.

impossible, and Fenstad liked that. He parked his car on a residential block[1] and took out his skates from the back seat, where he kept them all winter. With his fingertips he touched the wooden blade guards, thinking of the time. He checked his watch; he had fifteen minutes.

Out on the ice, still wearing his churchy[2] Sundaymorning suit, tie, and overcoat, but now circling the outside edge of the pond with his bare hands in his overcoat pockets, Fenstad admired the overcast sky and luxuriated[3] in the brittle cold. He was active and alert in winter but felt sleepy throughout the summer. He passed a little girl in a pink jacket, pushing a tiny chair over the ice. He waved to his friend Ann, an off-duty copracticing her twirls.[4] He waved to other friends. Without exception they waved back. As usual, he was impressed by the way skates improved human character.

Twenty minutes later, in the doorway of her apartment, his mother said, "Your cheeks are red." She glanced down at his trousers, damp with melted snow. "You've been skating." She kissed him on the cheek and turned to walk into her living room. "Skating after church? Isn't that some sort of error?[5]

"It's just happiness" Fenstad said. Quickly he checked her apartment for any signs of memory loss or depression. He found none and immediately felt relief. The apartment smelled of soap and Lysol,[6] the signs of an old woman who wouldn't tolerate nonsense. Out on her coffee table, as usual, were the letters she was writing to her congressman and to political dictators around the globe. Fenstad's mother pleaded for enlightened behavior and berated[7] the dictators for their bad political habits.

---

1) residential block : 주택지.
2) churchy : 교회갈 때 입는.
3) luxuriated : 즐겼다. to feel great enjoyment, to enjoy as luxury. cf. luxuriating in the warm sun.
4) twirl(s) : (급격하게 하는) 회전.
5) "Isn't that some sort of error?" : "좀 이상하지 않니?"
6) Lysol [lāisɔl] : 소독제.
7) berated : scolded.

She grasped the arm of the sofa and let herself down slowly. Only then did she smile. "How's your soul,[1] Harry?" she asked. "What's the news?"

He smiled back and smoothed his hair. Martin Luther King's[2] eyes locked into his from the framed picture on the wall opposite him. In the picture King was shaking hands with Fenstad's mother, the two of them surrounded by smiling faces. "My soul's okay, Ma," he said. "It's a hard project. I'm always working on it." He reached down for a chocolate-chunk cookie from a box on top of the television. "Who brought you these?"

"Your daughter Sharon. She came to see me on Friday." Fenstad's mother tilted her head at him."You want to be a good person, but she's the real article.[3] Goodness comes to her without any effort at all. She says you have a new girlfriend. A pharmacist this time. Susan, is it?" Fenstad nodded."Harry, why does your generation always have to find the right person? Why can't you learn to live with the wrong person? Sooner or later everyone's wrong. Love isn't the most important thing. Harry, far from it. Why can't you see that? I still don't comprehend why you couldn't live with Eleanor." Eleanor was Fenstad's ex-wife.[4] They had been divorced for a decade, but Fenstad's mother hoped for a reconciliation.

"come on, Ma"[5] Fenstad said. "Over and done with, gone and gone."[6] He took another cookie.

"You live with somebody so that you're living with somebody,[7] and then you go out and do the work of the world. I don't understand all this pickiness[8] about lovers.

---

1) soul =a seat of real life, vitality, or action.

2) Martin Luther King =Martin Luther King, Jr. (1929~68) 미국 흑인 인권운동의 지도자로서 1964년도 노벨 평화상을 받았으며, 1968년에 암살당했다.

3) the real article : 진짜 좋은 사람이나 물건.

4) ex-wife : 전처.

5) "Come on, Ma" 「엄마 그만두세요」

6) "Over and done with, gone and gone." 「Elenor와의 결혼이 벌써 옛날에 끝이 났어요?」

7) "You live with somebody so that you're living with somebody : 「어떤 사람과 살게 되면 그 결과 그 사람이 너에게 특별한 사람이 되는거다.」

8) pickiness : 까다로움 picky(미국영어) = excessively fastidious. Ex. a picky eater.

In a pinch[1] anybody'll do, Harry, believe me."

On the side table was a picture of her late husband[2], Fenstad's mild, middle-of-the-road[3] father. Fenstad glanced at the picture and let the silence hang between them before asking, "How are you, Ma?"

"I'm all right." She leaned back in the sofa, whose springs made a strange, almost human groan. "I want to get out. I spend too much time in this place in January. You should expand my horizons. Take me somewhere."

"Come to my composition class," Fenstad said. "I'll pick you up at dinnertime on Tuesday. Eat early"

"They'll notice me," she said, squinting. "I'm too old."

"I'll introduce you," her son said. "You'll fit right in."[4]

Fenstad wrote brochures in the publicity department[5] of a computer company during the day, and taught an extension English-composition class[6] at the downtown campus of the state university[7] two nights a week. He didn't need the money; he taught the class because he liked teaching strangers and because he enjoyed the sense of hope that classrooms held for him.[8] This hopefulness and didacticism[9] he had picked up from his mother.

On Tuesday night she was standing at the door of the retirement apartment building,[10] dressed in a dark blue overcoat—her best. Her stylishness was belied slightly by a pair of old fuzzy[11] red earmuffs. Inside the car Fenstad noticed that she had put on perfume, unusual for her. Leaning back, she gazed out contentedly at the

---

1) in a pinch =in time of difficulty or necessity.
2) her late husband =그녀의 세상떠난 남편.
3) middle-of-the road : (정책이나 정치가의) 중도(中道)의.
4) "You'll fit right in." : 「엄마는 곧 어울릴거예요」
5) publicity department : 홍보부.
6) an extention English-composition class : 대학의 영작문 공개강좌.
7) state university : 주립대학(교).
8) held for him : 그에게 좋았다.
9) didacticism : 계몽적인 교훈벽.
10) retirement apartment building : 퇴직한 노인용 아파트.
11) fuzzy : 털이 선.

nighttime lights.

"Who's in this group of students?" she asked. "Working-class people, I hope. Those are the ones you should be teaching. Anything else is just a career."[1]

"Oh, they work, all right." He looked at his mother and saw, as they passed under a streetlight, a combination of sadness and delicacy in her face. Her usual mask of tough optimism seemed to be deserting her.[2] He braked at a red light and said, "I have a hairdresser and a garage mechanic and a housewife, a Mrs. Nelson, and three guys who're sanitation workers.[3] Plenty of others. One guy you'll really like is a young black man with glasses who sits in the back row and reads Workers' Vanguard[4] and Bakunin [5]during class. He's brilliant. I don't know why he didn't test out of this class.[6] His name's York Follette, and he's — "

" I want to meet him," she said quickly. She scowled at the moonlit snow. "A man with ideas. People like that have gone out of my life." She looked over at her son. "What I hate about being my age is how nice everyone tries to be. I was never nice, but now everybody is pelting me with sugar cubes." She opened her window an inch and let the cold air blow over her, ruffling her stiff gray hair.

When they arrived at the school, snow had started to fall, and at the other end of the parking lot a police car's flashing light beamed long crimson rays through the dense flakes.[7] Fenstad's mother walked deliberately toward the door, shaking her head mistrustfully at the building and the police. Approaching the steps, she took her son's hand. "I liked the columns on the old buildings," she said, "the old university buildings, I mean. I liked Greek Revival[8] better than this Modernist-

---

1) career : (직업적인) 성공, 출세.
2) to be deserting her : (신념 등이) 그녀를 떠난다고.
3) sanitation worker(s) = sanitation man 청소국 직원.
4) *Workers' Vanguard* : 좌파의 주간 신문의 이름.
5) Bakunin [bəkúnin] = Mikhail Aleksandrovich Bakunin (1814~76) 러시아의 무정부 주의자 여기서는 버꾸닝이 쓴 책.
6) test out of this class.
7) dense flakes : 펴붓듯이 내리는 눈.
8) Greek Revival : 고대 희랍 양식 건물.

bunker stuff."[1] Inside, she blinked in the light at the smooth, waxed linoleum[2] floors and cemen-block walls. She held up her hand to shade her eyes. Fenstad took her elbow to guide her over the snow melting in puddles in the entryway.[3] "I never asked you what you're teaching tonight."

"Logic," Fenstad said.

"Ah." She smiled and nodded. "Dialectics!"[4]

"Not quite. Just logic."

She shrugged. She was looking at the clumps of students standing in the glare of the hallway,[5] drinking coffee from paper cups and smoking cigarettes in the general conversational din.[6] She wasn't used to such noise: she stopped in the middle of the corridor underneath a wall clock and stared happily in no particular direction. With her eyes shut she breathed in the close air,[7] smelling of wet overcoats and smoke, and Fenstad remembered how much his mother had always liked smoke - filled rooms, where ideas fought each other, and where some of those ideas died.

"Come on," he said, taking her hand again. Inside Fenstad's classroom six people sat in the angular postures of pre-boredom.[8] York Follette was already in the back row, his copy of Workers' Vanguard shielding his face. Fenstad's mother headed straight for him and sat down in the desk next to his. Fenstad saw them shake hands, and in two minutes they were talking in low, rushed[9] murmurs. He saw York Follette laugh quietly and nod. What was it that blacks saw and appreciated in his mother?[10] They had always liked her — written to her, called

---

1) this Modernist-bunker staff : 이런 현대풍의 큰 상자 같은 건물.
2) linoleum [linouliəm] : 리노륨.
3) entryway : 통로.
4) Dialectics : 헤겔의 변증법.
5) hallway : (미국) 낭하.
6) din = loud resonant and annoying noise.
7) the close [clous] air : (방의) 통풍이 안돼서 나쁜 공기.
8) pre-boredom : 권태를 느끼기 직전.
9) rushed : 서둔, 서두른
10) what was it that mother ? : 이것은 직접화법과 간접화법의 중간의 성질을 띤 묘출화법이다. cf. He wondered what it was that blacks saw and appreciated in his mother.

her, checked up on[1] her — and Fenstad wondered if they recognized something in his mother that he himself had never been able to see.

At 7:35 most of the students had arrived and were talking to each other vigorously, as if they didn't want Fenstad to start and thought they could delay him. He stared at them, and when they wouldn't quiet down, he made himself rigid and said,"Good evening. We have a guest tonight." Immediately the class grew silent. He held his arm out straight, indicating with a flick of his hand the old woman in the back row."My mother," he said."Clara Fenstad." For the first time all semester his students appeared to be paying attention: they turned around collectively and looked at Fenstad's mother, who smiled and waved. A few of the students began to applaud: others joined in. The applause was quiet but apparently genuine. Fenstad's mother brought herself slowly to her feet and made a suggestion of a bow. Two of the students sitting in front of her turned around and began to talk to her. At the front of the class Fenstad started his lecture on logic, but his mother wouldn't quiet down. This was a class for adults. They were free to do as they liked.

Lowering his head and facing the blackboard, Fenstad reviewed problems in logic, following point by point the outline set down[2] by the textbook: post hoc fallacies,[3] false authorities, begging the question, circular[4] reasoning, ad hominem arguments[5], all the rest. Explaining these problems, his back turned, he heard sighs of boredom, boldly expressed. Occasionally he glanced at the back of the room. His mother was watching him carefully, and her face was expressing all the complexity of dismay. Dismay radiated from her. Her disappointment wasn't personal, because his mother didn't think that people as individuals were at fault[6] for

---

1) check up on : examined.
2) set down : 제시된. set down앞에 which was가 생략됨.
3) *post hoc fallacies* : 인과(因果)의 허위. 시간적 전후 관계를 바로 인과관계와 동일시하는 오류(誤謬).
4) circular (논리) :「순환론적인」
5) ad hominem arguments : 대인입증. *ad hominem* [əd-hǽmənèm] : (의논시에) 이성보다는 상대의 감정이나 편견에 호소하는.
6) at fault : responsible.

what they did. As usual, her disappointed hope was located in history and in the way people agreed with already existing histories.

She was angry with him for collaborating with[1] grammar. She would call it unconsciously installed[2] authority. Then she would find other names for it.

"All right," he said loudly, trying to make eye contact with someone in the room besides his mother, "let's try some examples. Can anyone tell me what, if anything, is wrong with the following sentence? 'I, like most people, have a unique problem.'"

The three sanitation workers, in the third row, began to laugh. Fenstad caught himself glowering and singled out the middle one.

"Yes, it is funny, isn't it?"

The man in the middle smirked and looked at the floor. "I was just thinking of my unique problem."

"Right," Fenstad said. "But what's wrong with saying, 'I, like most people, have a unique problem'?"

"Solving it ?"[3] This was Mrs. Nelson, who sat by the window so that she could gaze at the tree outside, lit by a streetlight. All through class she looked at the tree as if it were a lover.

"Solving what?"

"Solving the problem you have. What is the problem?"

"That's actually not what I'm getting at,"[4] Fenstad said."Although it's a good related point. I'm asking what might be wrong logically with that setence."

"It depends," Harold Ronson said. He worked in a service station[5] and sometimes came to class wearing his work shirt with his name tag, HAROLD, stitched into it.[6] "It depends on what your problem is. You haven't told us your

1) collaborating with : 「동조하다」
2) installed : 설치된, 제정된.
3) "Solving it?" 그 문제를 해결하는데 말인가요? it =a unique problem.
4) getting at 〈 get at =insinuate.
5) service station : gas station.
6) stitched into it : 꿰맨. it =his work shirt.

problem."

"No," Festand said,"my problem is not the problem."[1] He thought of Alice in Wonderland[2] and felt, physically, as if he himself were getting small. "Let's try this again. What might be wrong with saying that most people have a unique problem?"

"You shouldn't be so critical,"[3] Timothy Melville said. "You should look on the bright side, if possible."

"What ?"

"He's right," Mrs. Nelson said. "Most people have unique problems, but many people do their best to help themselves, such as taking night classes or working at[4] meditation."

"No doubt that's true," Fenstad said. "But why can't most peope have a unique problem?"

"Oh, I disagree," Mrs. Nelson said, still looking at her tree. Fenstad glanced at it and saw that it was crested[5] with snow. It was beautiful. No wonder she looked at it. "I believe that most people do have unique problems. They just shouldn't talk about them all the time."

"Can anyone," Fenstad asked, looking at the back wall and hoping to see something there that was not wall,"can anyone give me an example of a unique problem?"

"Divorce," Barb Kjellerud said. She sat near the door and knitted during class. She answered questions without looking up. "Divorce is unique."

"No, it ins't!" Fenstad said, failing in the crucial moment to control his voice. He

---

1)"my problem is *not* the problem" : "나의 문제는 지금 관계가 없지요" 주인공 Fenstad는 어떻게 해서든지 "Most people"의 "most"와 "unique"가 논리적으로 양립하지 않는다는 것을 입증하려 한다.

2) Alice in Wonderland : 영국작가 Lewis Carroll (1832~98) 저서의 *Alice's Adventures in Wonderland* (1885)의 주인공. 이 어린 주인공은 꿈속에서 파라독스나 넌센스가 가득한 불가사의의 나라를 여행한다.

3) critical : looking for faults. cf. of or at a crisis.

4) working at- 〉 work at- : (-에) 골몰하다. cf. at work =working; at one's place of employment.

5) crested =covered.

and his mother exchanged glances. In his mother's face for a split second[1] was the history[2] of her compassionate, ambivalent attention to him. "Divorce is not unique. " He waited to calm himself. "It's everywhere. Now try again. Give me a unique problem."

Silence. "This is a trick question."[3] Arlene Hubbly said. "I'm sure it's a trick question"

"Not necessarily. Does anyone know what unique[4] means?"

"One of a kind,"[5] York Follette said, gazing at Fenstad with dry amusement. Sometimes he took pity on Fenstad and helped him out of jams. Fenstad's mother smiled and nodded.

"Right," Fenstad crowed,[6] racing toward the blackboard as if he were about to write something. "So let's try again. Give me a unique problem."

"You give us a unique problem." one of the sanitation workers said. Fenstad didn't know whether he'd been given a statement or a command. He decided to treat it as a command.

"All fight,"he said. He stopped and looked down at his shoes. Maybe it was a trick question. He thought for ten seconds. Problem after problem presented itself to him.He thought of poverty, of the assaults on the earth, of the awful complexities of love. "I can't think of one," Fenstad said. His hands went into his pockets.

"That's because problems aren't personal," Fenstad's mother said from the back of the room. "They're collective." She waited while several students in the class sat up[1] and nodded. "And people must work together on their solutions." She talked for another two minutes, taking the subject out of logic and putting it neatly in politics, where she knew it belonged.

---

1) a split second . 「한순간」 split는 분할하다의 뜻.
2) was the history : 도치되었음.
3) a trick question : 골탕을 먹이려는 문제(질문).
4) *unique* = being the only one of its kind., Ex. *This race is unique.* 때로 unusual, remarkable의 뜻도 있다.
5) "One of a kind" : 「같은 종류중의 하나」
6) crowed 〈 crow : 「(의기양양해서) 기뻐하다」

The snow had stopped by the time the class was over. Fenstad took his mother's arm and escorted her to the car. After letting her down[2] on the passenger side and starting the engine, he began to clear[3] the front windshield. He didn't have a scraper[4] and had forgotten his gloves, so he was using his bare hands. When he brushed the snow away on his mother's side, she looked out at him, surprised, a terribly aged Sleeping Beauty[5] awakened against her will.

Once the car had warmed up, she was in a gruff mood and repositioned[6] herself under the seat belt while making quiet but aggressive remarks. The sight of the new snow didn't seem to calm her. "Logic," she said at last. "That wasn't logic. Those are just rhetorical tactic.[7] It's filler[8] and drudgery."

"I don't want to discuss it now."

"All right. I'm sorry. Let's talk about somethig more pleasant."

They rode together in silence. Then she began to shake her head. "Don't take me home," she said. "I want to have a spot of tea[9] somewhere before I go back. A nice place where they serve tea, all right?"

He parked outside an all - night restaurant with huge front plate-glass[10] windows; it was called Country Bob's. He held his mother's elbow from the car to the door. At the door, looking back to make sure that he had turned off his headlights, he saw his tracks[11] and his mother's in the snow. His were separate footprints, but hers

---

1) sat up 〈 sit up : 바로 앉다.

2) After letting her down : 「자리에 앉힌 다음」 passenger side = passenger seat 「(특히 자동차의) 조수석 또는 운전기사의 옆자리」

3) clear : 「깨끗하게 닦다」

4) scraper : 여기서는 차의 앞 유리에 쌓인 눈을 치우는 딱딱한 고무가 달린 스크레퍼.

5) The Sleeping Beauty : 「잠자는 (숲속의) 미녀」 프랑스 작가 Perrault의 요정 이야기. Robert Samber가 1729년에 번역. 잠자는 미녀는 태양의 빛에 의해 겨울잠에서 깨어나는 대지를 비유한다.

6) repositioned 〈 reposition : 「~의 위치를 변경하다」

7) rhetorical tactics : 수사학적 전술 (술책), 말장난.

8) filler : 「시간 때우기」

9) a spot of tea (영국영어) = a cup of tea.

10) plate-glass : 「판유리」

11) tracks : 발자국. his mother's = his mother's tracks.

formed two long lines.

Inside, at the table, she sipped her tea and gazed at her son for a long time. "Thanks for the adventure, Harry. I do appreciate it. What're you doing in class next week? Oh, I remember. How - to papers ?[1] That should be interesting."

"Want to come?"

"Very much. I'll keep quiet next time, if you want me to."

Fenstad shook his head."It's okay.[2] It's fun having you along. You can say whatever you wnat. The students loved you. I knew you'd be a sensation, and you were. They'd probably rather have you teaching the class than me."

He noticed that his mother was watching something going on behind him, and Fenstad turned around in the booth so that he could see what it was. At first all he saw was a woman, a young woman with long hair wet from snow and hanging in clumps,[3] talking in the aisle to two young men, both of whom were nodding at her. Then she moved on to the next table. She spoke softly. Fenstad couldn't hear her words, but he saw the solitary customer to whom she was speaking shake his head once, keeping his eyes down. Then the woman saw Fenstad and his mother. In a moment she was standing in front of them.

She wore two green plaid[4] flannel shirts and a thin torn jacket. Like Fenstad, she wore no gloves. Her jeans were patched, and she gave off[5] a strong smell, something like hay, Fenstad thought, mixed with tar and sweat. He looked down at her feet and saw that she was wearing penny loafers[6] with no socks. Coins, old pennies, were in both shoes; the leather was wet and cracked. He looked in the woman's face. Under a hat that seemed to collapse on either side of her head, the

---

1) How-to papers : 어떤 일을 하는 방법에 관해서 설명하는 레포트(보고서).
2) It's okay : 「(조용히 하지 않아도) 좋아요」
3) in clumps =in clusters.
4) plaid [plæd] : 「격자무늬의」
5) gave off 〈 give off : 「(증기, 냄새, 빛 등을) 배출하다, 발산하다.」
6) penny loafers = informal loafers (발뒤꿈치가 없는 산달식의 가죽신) that have leather slots in front in which a penny or other coin in placed.

woman's face was thin and chalk - white except for the fatigue lines[1] under her eyes. The eyes themselves were bright blue, beautiful, and crazy. To Fenstad, she looked desperate, percolating[2] slightly with insanity, and he was about to say so to his mother when the woman bent down toward him and said, "Mister, can you spare any money?"[3]

Involuntarily, Fenstad looked toward the kitchen, hoping that the manager would spot this person and take her away. When he looked back again, his mother was taking her blue coat off, wriggling in the booth to free her arms from the sleeves. Stopping and starting again, she appeared to be stuck inside the coat; then she lifted herself up, trying to stand, and with a quick, quiet groan slipped the coat off.[4] She reached down and folded the coat over and held it toward the woman. "Here," she said. "Here's my coat. Take it before my son stops me."

"Mother, you can't." Fenstad reached forward to grab the coat, but his mother pulled it away from him.

When Fenstad looked back at the woman, her mouth was open, showing several gray teeth. Her hands were outstretched, and he understood, after a moment, that this was a posture of refusal, a gesture saying no, and that the woman wasn't used to it and did it awkwardly. Fenstad's mother was standing and trying to push the coat toward the woman, not toward her hands but lower, at waist level, and she was saying, "Here, here, here, here." The sound, like a human birdcall, frightened Fenstad, and he stood up quickly, reached for his wallet, and removed the first two bills he could find, two twenties.[5] He grabbed the woman's chapped, ungloved left hand.

"Take these", he said, putting the two bills in her icy palm, "for the love of God, and please go."

---

1) the fatigue lines : 「피로때문에 생긴 주름살」
2) percolating 〈 percolate : 「활기를 보이다」
3) spare any money : 「돈을 주다, 나누어 주다」
4) slipped (the coat) off : 「(의복같은 것을) 슬쩍 벗다」
5) two twenties : 「20불짜리 지폐 2장」

He was close to her face. Tonight he would pray for her. For a moment the woman's expression was vacant .His mother was still pushing the coat at her, and the woman was unsteadily[1] bracing[2] herself. The woman's mouth was open, and her stagnant - water breath[3] washed over him."I know you," she said. "You're my little baby cousin."

"Go away, lease," Fenstad said. He pushed at her.[4] She turned, clutching his money. He reached around to put his hands on his mother's shoulders. "Ma," he said, "she's gone now. Mother, sit down. I gave her money for a coat." His mother fell down on her side of the booth, and her blue coat rolled over on the bench beside her, showing the label and the shiny inner lining.[5] When he looked up, the woman who had been begging had disappeared, though he could still smell her odor, an essence of wretchedness.[6]

"Excuse me, Harry," his mother said. "I have to go to the bathroom."

She rose and walked toward the front of the restaurant, turned a corner, and was out of sight. Fenstad sat and tried to collect himself.[7] When the waiter came, a boy with an earring and red hair in a flattop,[8] Fenstad just shook his head and said, "More tea." He realized that his mother hadn't taken off her earmuffs, and the image of his mother in the ladies' room with her earmuffs on[9] gave him a fit of uneasiness.[10] After getting up from the booth and following the path that his mother had taken, he stood outside the ladies' room door and, when no one came in or out, he knocked.

---

1) unsteadily : 비틀거리면서.
2) bracing 〈 brace : 「(쓰러지지않도록) 발에 힘을 주다」
3) stagnant-water breath : 「고인물같은 (썩은) 숨결」
4) pushed at her : 「그녀를 밀려고 했다」 cf. pushed her.
5) the shiny inner lining. : 광태있는 안감.
6) an essence of wretchedness : 「비참한 상태 그 자체」 이것은 her odor를 다시 설명하는 동격적 표현.
7) collect himself : 「자신을 가다듬다」 =(to) regain control of himself.
8) flattop : 「(원래는 aircraft carrier 항공모함) 평평하게 깎은 상고머리」
9) with her earmuffs on 은 the image를 수식한다.
10) a fit of uneasiness 갑작스런 불안감
fit는 명사로서 감정의 격발을 의미.

He waited for a decent[1] interval. Still hearing no answer, he opende the door.

His mother was standing with her arms down on either side of the first sink.[2] She was holding herself there, her eyes following the hot water as it poured from the tap[3] around the bright porcelain sink down into the drain, and she looked furious. Fenstad touched her and she snapped toward him.

"Your logic!" she said.

He opened the door for her and helped her back to the booth. The second cup of tea had been served, and Fenstad's mother sipped it in silence. They did not converse. When she had finished, she said, "All right. I do feel better now. Let's go."

At the curb in front of her apartment building he leaned forward and kissed her on the cheek. "Pick me up next Tuesday," she said. "I want to go back to that class." He nodded. He watched as she made her way[4] past the security guard[5] at the front desk; then he put his car into drive and started home.

That night he skated in the dark for an hour with his friend Susan, the pharmacist. She was an excellent skater; they had met on the ice. She kept late hours[6] and, like Fenstad, enjoyed skating at night. She listened attentively to his story about his mother and the woman in the restaurant. To his great relief she recommended no course of action. She listened. She didn't believe in[7] giving advice, even when asked.

The following Tuesday, Fenstad's mother was again in the back row next to York Follette. One of the fluorescent lights overhead was flickering, which gave the room, Fenstad thought, a sinister quality, like a debtors' prison or a refuge for the

---

1) decent : (구어)「상당한, 꽤 오랜」 cf. earn a *decent* salary (= quite good)
2) sink = a fixed basin with a drainage pipe and usually with a water supply, in a kitchen, etc. (화장실 세면대)
3) tap = 수도꼭지.
4) made her way 〈 make one's way : 「나아가다」
5) security guard = security man (경비원).
6) kept late hours 〈 keep late hours : 「늦은 시간까지 깨어있다」
7) believe in : 「~의 가치를 믿다」

homeless. He'd been thinking about such people for the entire week. For seven days now he had caught whiffs of the woman's breath[1] in the air, and one morning, Friday, he thought he caught a touch of the rotten - celery smell on his own breath, after a particularly difficult sales meeting.

Tonight was how - to night.[2] The students were expected to stand at the front of the class and read their papers, instructing their peers[3] and answering questions if necessary. Starting off, and reading her paper in a frightened monotone, Mrs. Nelson told the class how to bake a cheese soufflé. Arlene Hubbly's paper was about mushroom hunting. Fenstad was put off[4] by the introduction. "The advantage to mushrooms" Arlene Hubbly read, "is that they are delicious. The disadvantage to mushrooms, in that they can make you sick, even die." But then she explained how to recognize the common shaggymane[5] by its cylindrical cap and dark tufts; she drew a model on the board.[6] She warned the class against the Clitocybe illudens, the Jack-o'-Lantern.[7] "Never eat a mushroom like this one or any mushroom that glows in the dark. Take heed!" she said, fixing her gaze on the class. Fenstad saw his mother taking rapid notes. Harold Ronson, the mechanic, reading his own prose plainfully and slowly, told the class how to get rust spots out of their automobiles. Again Fenstad noticed his mother taking notes. York Follette told the class about the proper procedures for laying down attic insulation and how to know when enough was enough, so that a homeowner wouldn't be robbed blind, as he put it,[8] by the salesmen, in whose ranks he had once counted himself.

---

1) whiffs of the woman's breath : 「그 여인에게서 풍기는 숨결」
2) how-to night : 「"how-to papers"를 공부하는 밤」
3) peers : 「동료들」
4) was put off ＜ put off : 「(사람의) 의욕을 잃게하다」 to dissuade. cf. The smell puts me off.
5) shaggymane : 「식용버섯」
6) board =blackboard.
7) *Clitocybe illudens*, the Jack-o'-Lantern : 「일종의 빛이 나는 버섯」 Clitocybe illudens는 라틴어로 된 학명.
8) as he put it : 「그분의 말로는」

Barb Kjellerud had brought along a cassette player, and told the class that her hobby was ballroom dancing; she would instruct them in the basic waltz. She pushed the play button on the tape machine, and Tales from the Vienna Woods[1] came booming out. To the accompaniment of the music she read her paper, illustrating, as she went, how the steps were to be performed. She danced alone in front of them, doing so with flair.[2] Her blond hair swayed as she danced, Fenstad noticed. She looked a bit like a contestant in a beauty contest who had too much personality to win. She explained to the men the necessity of leading. Someone had to lead, she said, and tradition had given this responsibility to the male. Fenstad heard his mother snicker.

When Barb Kjellerud asked for volunteers, Fenstad's mother raised her hand. She said she knew how to waltz and would help out. At the front of the calss she made a counterclockwise motion with her hand, and for the next minute, sitting[3] at the back of the room, Fenstad watche his mother and one of the sanitation workers waltzing under the flickering fluorescent lights.

"What a wonderful class," Fenstad's mother said on the way home. "I hope you're paying attention to what they tell you."

Fenstad nodded. "Tea?" he asked.

She shook her head."Where're you going after you drop me off?"

"Skating," he said. "I usually go skating. I have a date."

"With the pharmacist? In the dark?"

"We both like it, Ma." As he drove, he made an all-purpose[4] gesture. "The moon and the stars." he said simply.

---

1) *Tales from the Vienna Woods* : 「비엔나 숲의 이야기」(1866) Johann Strauss (1825~99)가 작곡한·왈츠.

2) with flair : (구어) 「멋지게」 flair =a natural ability to do something well or to select and recognize what is good or useful etc. Do not confuse *flair* with *flare*.

3) sitting의 주어는 Fenstad.

4) all-purpose : 「어떤 의미로도 사용되는」

When he left her off,[1] he felt unsettled. He considered, as a point of courtesy, staying with her a few minutes, but by the time he had this idea he was already away from the building and was headed down the street.

He and Susan were out on the ice together, skating in large circles, when pointed to a solitary figure sitting on a park bench near the lake's edge. The sky had cleared; the moon gave everything a cold, fine - edged[2] clarity. When Fenstad followed the line of Susan's finger, he saw at once that the figure on the bench was his mother. He realized it simply because of the way she sat there, drawn into herself,[3] attentive even in the winter dark. He skated through the uncleared snow over the ice until he was standing close enough to speak to her. "Mother," he said, "What are you doing here?"

She was bundled up, a thick woolen cap drawn over her head, and two scarves covering much of her face. He could see little other than the two lenses of her glasses facing him in the dark. "I wanted to see you two," she told him. "I thought you'd look happy, and you did. I like to watch happiness. I always have."

"How can you see us? We're so far away."

"That's how I saw you."

This made no sense to him, so he asked, "How'd you get here?"

"I took a cab. That part was easy."

"Aren't you freezing?"

"I don't know. I don't know if I'm freezing or not."

He and Susan took her back to her apartment as soon as they could get their boots on. In the car Mrs. Fenstad insisted on asking Susan what kind of safety procedures were used to ensure that drugs[4] weren't smuggled out of pharmacies and sold illegally, but she didn't appear to listen to the answer, and by the time they reached

---

1) left her off 〈 leave off : 어머니를 차에서 내려 드리다.
2) fine-edged : 「예리한」
3) drawn into herself 〈 draw : 자기 자신속으로 움츠리고.
4) drugs : 「불법적인 마약들」

her building, she seemed to be falling asleep. They helped her up to her apartment. Susan thought that they should give her a warm bath before putting her into bed, and, together, they did. She did not protest. She didn't even seem to notice them as they guided her in and out of the bathtub.

Fenstad feared that his mother would catch some lung infection,[1] and it turned out to be bronchitis, which kept her in her apartment for the first three weeks of February, until her cough went down.[2] Fenstad came by every other day to see how she was, and one Tuesday, after work, he went up her floor and heard piano music: and old recording, which sounded much played, of the brightest and fastest jazz piano he had ever heard — music of superhuman brilliance. He swung open[3] the door to her apartment and saw York Follette sitting near his mother's bed. On the bedside table was a small tape player, from which the music poured into the room.

Fenstad's mother was leaning back against the pillow, smiling, her eyes closed.

Follette turned toward Fenstad. He had been talking softly. He motioned toward the tape machine and said. "Art Tatum.[4] It's cut[5] called 'Battery Bounce.'[6] Your mother's never heard it."

"Jazz, Harry," Fenstad's mother said, her eyes still closed, not needing to see her son. "York is explaingin to me about Art Tatum and jazz. Next week he's going to try something more progressive on me." Now his mother opened her eyes. "Have you ever heard such music before, Harry?"

They were both looking at him. "No," he said, "I never heard anything like it."

"This is my unique problem, Harry." Fenstad's mother coughed and then waited to

---

1) lung infection : 「폐의 감염」
2) went down < go down : 「진정되다」
3) Swung open < Swing open : 「문이 활짝 흔들리다, 열리다」 cf. *in full swing* = with activity at its greatest. *Swinging door* = a door that opens in either direction and closes itself when released.
4) Art Tatum : Ohio주 태생의 재즈 피아니스트 (1909~1956)
5) cut : 「레코드판, 또는 레코드에 곡을 컷한 레코드 명」
cf. cut = the cutting out of part of a play or film, etc.
6) Battery Bounce : Art Tatum이 1941년에 발표한 레코드명.

recover her breath.[1] "I never heard enough jazz." She smiled, "What glimpses!" she said at last.

After she recovered, he often found her listening to the tape machine that York Follette had given her. She liked to hear the Oscar Peterson Trio[2] as the sun set and the lights of evening came on. She now often mentioned glimpses. Back at home, every night, Fenstad spoke about his mother in his prayers of remembrance and thanksgiving, even though he knew she would disapprove.

---

1) recover her breath : 「제대로 숨을 쉬다」
2) Oscar Peterson Trio : 몬트리올 태생의 재즈 피아니스트 (1925~). Peterson Trio는 피아노, 기타, double bass를 사용하였으나 (1953~58), 후에 기타는 drum으로 바뀌었다(1959~65).

1. * It's Off to Work We Go[1]

I woke up one morning and thought I'd eat an orange.

"Are you sure you want to do that?"[2] my wife asked.

"Why not?"

"They could be from Chile. Somebody from Chile wants to kill us."

"You're right. I think I'll have an apple instead."

She threw herself down on her knees.[3] "Please don't eat an apple. What will happen to all of us if you eat an apple?"

"How selfisch of me," I said. "I have no right to consume an apple when so many people depend on me. Any late bulletins on shredded wheat?"[4]

"None so far,[5] but that doesn't mean the milk doesn't have pesticides[6] in it. I just read an article which said that cows are ingesting all kinds of poisons in their foods. You'd be a fool to take a chance."[7]

"Then I'll have a slice of bread and a cup of coffee."

My wife told me, "Marie Hawke says coffee causes cancer in rats."

"Has she ever seen a rat with cancer?"

---

* 음식물은 오염되었으며 그에 의해 질병에 걸릴 수도 있다. 집밖에 나가면 어떤 재앙이 닥칠지 알길이 없다.

1) "It's off to work we go" : 「자아, 일하러 갑시다.」

2) to do that = to eat an orange.

3) threw herself down on her knees 〈 throw oneself down on one's knees : 무릎을 꿇고' 애원했다.

4) Any late bulletins on shredded wheat?

5) so far : 「지금까지는, 아직은」

6) pesticides : 「살충제」

7) to take a chance = to take a risk, to act in the hope that a particular thing will (or will not) happen. cf. (to) take chances = to behave riskily. (to) take one's chances = to trust to luck.

No, but Geraldo Rivera[1] has, and he showed the rat on TV the other night."

"So much for breakfast. I guess I'll be off to work."

"You're not going to drive on the Beltway?"[2] she gasped.

"What's wrong with that?"

"There is ten times as much hazardous waste being transported on the highway now as there was two years ago. One trailer spill and you'll be in cruise control with the angels."[3]

"That's not a very comforting thought. But we can't be intimidated by hazardous - waste trucks. They would like nothing more than for us to stay home so that they can have the highways to themselves."

I put on my driving golves.

"Suppose you get shot," she cried, blocking the door with her body.

"I'm not going to get shot," I assured her. "Nobody wants to shoot me."

"It's happening to people in Washington every day. Don't you ever watch Dan Rather[4] on television?"

"The odds are still in my favor.[5] I'm going to stay out of the neighborhoods where the shootings take place."

"So let's say[6] you make it[7] to the office. What about the asbestos[8] in your ceiling?" she asked. "Doesn't that make you think twice about going to work?"

"I'm in a new building. It's been inspected."

"What are your plans for the lunch hour?"

"I'm not sure yet, why?"

---

1) Geraldo Rivera : 「제랄도 리베라」 "Good Morning America," "Entertainment Tonight"등 토크쇼의 호스트, 저널리스트.
2) Beltway : Washinton D.C. 주변의 환상도로(순환도로).
3) you'll be in cruise control with the angels =you will die. "be in cruise control" 「쾌속주행의 상태로 달리다」
4) Dan Rather : 「단래더」 CBS Evening News의 선임 앵커맨.
5) The odds are still in my favor : 「그래도 나는 문제 없어」
6) let's say =suppose.
7) make it : 어찌어찌해서 도착하다.
8) asbestos : 「아스베스도:석면」 발암성 물질.

"Whatever you do, don't take a flight to Europe. The PLO[1] is threatening to hijack a plane."

"I'm glad you warned me. I probably would have flown to Shannon[2] for corned beef and cabbage. Anything else I should be on the lookout for?"

"The air is supposed to be foul today. I wouldn't go jogging if I were you, and don't stare at your computer screen too long or you'll go blind."

"Was that on the 'Today'[3] show?"

"No, '60 Minutes.'"[4]

"I got it. So what aren't we going to have for dinner tonight?"

"We're not eating any fish until they stop spawning in acid rain."

"Enough chitchat.[5] Give me my construction worker's helmet and a kiss and I'll be off."

She hugged me as June Allyson[6] always does in her pictures and whispered, "Have a nice day."

---

1) PLO =Palestine Liberation Organization :「팔레스티나 해방기구」

2) Shanon :「샤논」 아일랜드 서부의 국제공항.

3) 'Today' : NBC에서 아침 7시에 하는 인기 뉴스 쇼로서 다년간 방송되고 있다.

4) '60 munutes' . 일요일에 방영되는 시청률이 높은 보도프로. 앵커가 집요하게 사건을 추적하여 관계자들에게 가차없는 인터뷰를 강요하며, 그 내용을 카메라가 냉혹하게 포착보도하는 식의 수사보도(investigative report)의 모범을 보인 프로이다.

5) chitchat =n.chat, gossip.

6) June Allyson :「쥰 앨리슨」 텔런트 겸 영화배우.

2. Wrong Number*

Ever since they broke up the phone company people seem to be showered with wrong numbers.

I believe there calls are not accidental but are placed[1] by a syndicate[2] of perverts[3] stationed in boiler rooms around the country. The purpose of the wrong - number dialer is to ring up when a person least expects it and cause the victim to break his toe on an end table.[4]

What is the payoff[5] for someone making a wrong - number call? It gives the dialer a sense of power he or she never had before, and a way for many of the callers to get even with their mothers.[5]

This is how the team assigned to my house works: The first dialer rings only at bathtime. I can't afford to ignore the phone because it might be Ed McMahon[6] telling me I won ten million dollars in a sweepstakes,[7] so I slosh[8] across the floor and pick up the receiver. At which point[9] the caller hangs up. Like all idiots who

---

* 세계최대의 전화회사는 미국전화통신회사(AT&T)였다. 1987년에 22개였던 벨 전화회사(Bell Operating Companies)를 분할하여 기업재편성을 행했다. 그 결과 다음과 같은 유우머와 풍자가 나왔다.

1) are place 〈 place : (교환을 통해서) 전화를 걸다.
2) syndicate [sindikeit] : (범죄)조직. cf. an association of people or firms combining to carry out business or commertial undertaking.
3) end table = a small table, usually placed alongside an end of a couch or beside a chair. cf. end product.
4) pay off = payment, reward or retribution, a climax, especially of a joke or story.
5) get even with their mothers : 「어머니에게 앙갚음하다」(어머니가 하지 말라는 짓을 고의로 하여 어머니를 괴롭히는 어린이들의 장난.)
6) Ed McMahon : TV 아나운서.
7) sweepstakes : 「상금내기, 추첨」
8) slosh : 「물을 튀기면서 걷다.」 = to move with a splashing sound.
9) At which point : at that moment.

receive wrong numbers I keep screaming "hello!" into the phone until I realize it is futile. I return the receiver to the cradle and say to my wife, "How could he know I was in the bath?" My wife replies, "That's not the question. The question is, how did he know you'd get out of the bath?"

My second caller has a thick accent and it wouldn't surprise me if he was in the country illegally. Here's how this wrong call goes:

"Hello, Sam," he says.

"This is not Sam. There is no Sam in this house."

"Who you?"[1]

"I'm the person who owns the phone. You have the wrong number."

"You tell Sam he better call me or I smash his face in."

"Okay, I'll tell him," I say. "But you still have the wrong number."

"You tell Sam I'm going to smash him in his face for giving me the wrong number."

One of my other dialers sounds like a kid. Those calls go like this: "Grandpa?"

"Yes, this is Grandpa. Is this Jason?"

"No, it's Nicholas. You're not my grandpa."

"You're right. You shouldn't use the phone when your parents aren't there."

"My daddy's right here."

"What are you bothering my kid for?"[2] a man's voice says.

"If he's for real,[3] which I doubt, he called my number by mistake."

"Then why did you answer the phone? He's only five years old."

While I get my share of wrong numbers during the waking hours, I have observed that most of the calls come very early in the morning. They are made by people who sound just like teenagers, and they get extremely angry at me when they find out they're not talking to Bubba.[4]

If you tell the person on the phone you don't know where Bubba is, they accuse

---

1) "who you?" ="who are you?"
2) "What are you bothering my kid for?" ="Why are you bothering my kid?"
3) "If he's for real" ="If he is being honest"
4) Bubba [bʌ́bə] : 남자이름. 때때로 무식하고 단순한 사람에게 사용되는 이름.

you of locking him in the furnace room, which you had no right to do.

There is only one thing worse than a Bubba caller and that's a heavy breather,[1] who checks in at three o'clock in the morning. The first time he started breathing I handed the receiver to my wife and said, "It's for you."

"How do you know? It could be a woman."

"Do you think there are female heavy breathers?"

She rolled over and said, "Why don't you ask her?"

This is just a sample of my wrong-number callers. There are only two conclusions you can come to about why they are so numerous. One is, there are a lot more crazy people in the country than the census shows; and the other is, the telephone lines are even more fouled up than anyone imagines.

1) a heavy breather : 일종의 변태자.

3. This War Is the Battle of the Couches*

At the begining of the Persian Gulf war[1] we all sat quietly on our couches[2] and left the fighting to the network anchormen.[3]

We also deferred to[4] the wisdom of the retired military experts hired to guide us through the mine fields.[5]

But as the days and nights wore on, Americans became battle -savvy[6] and, and with football fans, they all started developing their own opinions as to how the game should be fought.

Suddenly, the generals' strategy was being questioned by the man in the street, and there were rumblings that those giving the briefings did not know what they were talking about.

I first sensed skepticism when my taxi driver said, "You know what we ought to be doing. We should find Hussein's[7] bunker[8] and drop a 1,000 -pound delayed bomb[9] loaded with TNT down his chimney. It has 30 seconds to go off, and if

---

* 페르샤만의 전쟁때, 소파에 앉아서 TV만 보는 소위 "카우치 포테이토"들은 자신들이 전쟁에 정통한 군사령관이 된 기분으로 전황을 논한다.

1) the Persian Gulf war : 페르샤만 전쟁.
2) couch(es) = a sofa or settee.
cf. = to express in words of a certain kind. Ex. *The reques was couched in polite terms.*
3) network anchorman : (뉴스보도의) 「캐스터」
4) deferred to - > derer to - = to put off to a later time, to postpone, to yield, to give way to a person's wishes or judgement or authority.
5) mine field(s) : 「지뢰매설장(들)」
6) battle-savvy [sǽvi(:)] : 전투에 정통한.
savvy = n. (slang) common sense, understanding.
7) Hussein : 「후세인」 이라크의 대통령.
8) bunker : 「엄호속의 지휘소」
9) delayed bomb : 「지연폭탄」 TNT 화약.

Hussein doesn't give up Kuwait, we will drive a stake through his heart."

"That's a good idea," I told him.

"Then how come Tom Brokaw[1] never thought of it?"

"He's been dealing with the Scud missile[2] problem, and he can't think of everything."

"If you solve the Hussein question, you don't have a Scud problem."

"You sound as if you know a lot about the military situation. Were you in the service[3]?" I asked.

"No, but my brother was a truck driver in Korea."

When I reached the office, I found Bob Goodier[4] studying a map of Kuwait at The Washington Post. "This is where we make our next move," he yelled, bringing his thumb down on a spot in the desert.

"Have you checked it with Dan Rater?"[5]

"What he doesn't know won't hurt him", Bob chuckled.

"But you can't call for a military operation without having at least two of the four networks approving."

Goodier said, "This is no longer an anchorman's war. It's a couch potato's [6] war and we call the shots."[7]

"You really want to open up the front in Kuwait now?"

"What if Eisenhower[8] had hesitated to invade on D -day?[9]" he asked.

---

1) Tom Brokaw : 「톰 부로꼬」 미국 NBC의 "Prime Time" 의 뉴스해설자 (앵커맨).
2) Scud missile : 「스커드 미사일」 이라크가 이스라엘과 사우디아라비아에 발사했던 소련제 미사일.
3) in the service : 「군에서 복무하는, 군대에 있는」
4) Bob Goodier : 「같은 사무실에서 일하는 직원」
5) Dan Rather : 「단래더」 미국 CBS의 "Evening News"의 대표 앵커맨.
6) couch potato : (유행어) 「카우치 포테이토」 포테이토 칩같은 것을 먹으면서 소파에 앉아 하염없이 텔리비전을 보는 사람.
7) we call the shots =we call for military operations.
8) Eisenhower : 「아이젠 하우어」 (1890~1969) 제 34대 미국 대통령 ('53~'61)
9) D-day : 「(제2차 세계대전중에 1944년 6월 6일에 있은 영미연합군에 의한) 북부 프랑스 공격개시일」 독일군의 패배를 초래했다.

"He had no choice. George Will[1] wasn't there to tell him what to do. Look, there's a danger in letting the couch potatoes run the war."

"Then why do they allow us to watch it on the tube? We cannot be expected to sit there and just suck our thumbs when there is so much bombing to be done."

"All America wants[2] is for us to be a well - informed public. We can't call the shots as well."

"It doesn't take a couch potato long to know how to shoot down an Iraqi fighter plane."

"Goodier, you have to leave the fighting to Peter Jennings."[3]

"It's like watching football ad not being able to tell the coach how to run the team."

"What do you think we should do?"

"I think we should drive a stake[4] into Hussein's heart."

"That's strange."

"What's strange?"

"You're the second person who suggested that today."

---

1) George Will : 「죠지윌」 뉴스해설자. 정치칼럼집필자. ABC의 "This Week"에 출연.

2) All America wants : 「미국이 원하는 것은 다만」 all 다음에 that 가 생략됨. cf. all-American = adj. typically American, chosen as best in any U.S. port. all-American = n. an all-American player.

3) Peter Jennings : 「피터 제닝스」 ABC의 유명한 앵커맨.

4) drive a stake : 말뚝을 박다.

4. The Truth, the Whole Truth*

The only thing you see when world leaders meet is their exit. All you hear are pallid[1] declarations as the leaders face the microphones.

"We had a very fruitful exchange[2] which will eventually lead to mutual undestanding," the Premier[3] says.

The U.S. Secretary of State[4] then speaks. "The discussions were frank and open and we hope someday they will produce positive results for the entire region."

Diplomacy demands the two people make such statements. But you have to read between the lines[5] to get the real meaning.

This is what the Premier really wished to say when he described the talks as fruitful. "When the Secretary of State tried to blackmail me by threatening to cut off ground-to-air missile deliveries,[6] I had no choice but to throw the fruit bowl at him."

While the Scretary of State really wanted to say, "What can you expect from a man who has devoted his entire life to being short?"[7]

And so it goes. Here is the dialogue — and what the leaders were really thinking:

The Premier speaks into the mikes, "We had sharp exchanges but now we can move forward." ("The Secretary wants peace and he wants the Russians at the table. How can he have both? The trouble with the American is he plays too much tennis and the sun gets to his head.")

"I want to say," the Secretary of State declares, "the areas of agreement are far greater than those of disagreement. I have gotten to know the Premier better and

---

* 외교에 있어 양국대표들의 공언과 그들의 저의에는 크나큰 차이가 있다.

1) pallid [pæ̀lid] =dull.
2) exchange : 「의견교환」
3) Premier [primiə] =Prime Minister.
4) Secretary of State : (미국) 「국무장관」
5) read between the lines : 행간의 의미를 읽다. 숨은 뜻을 알아내다.
6) ground-to-air-missile deliveries : 「地對空 미사일 발사장치」
7) has devoted ~ to being short : 일생동안 말을 간략하게 해왔다.

that was worth my entire trip." ("If I had seen how little I was going to get out of all this I would have brought De Tocqueville[1] with me and stayed in the hotel.")

The Premier is next. "Two great nations can agree to disagree, but this should not stop them from supplying each other with helicopters." ("Not only is the American Secretary of State wrong on everything — he is also boring. Anyone who can put my entire cabinet to sleep with his final peace offer deserves a Nobel peace prize.")

The Secretary, not to be outdone,[2] asserts, "I intend to come back and continue the discussions we have had today, because only by talking across the table will we be able to reach solutions to knotty problems that confront the Premier and myself." ("Even if he agreed to everything, I could not accept the terms because I did not understand a word he was saying")

World leaders know their remarks will be shown on television and sent around the world. That's why they don't want to look like losers.

The Premier has a lot going on in his head when he is speaking into the mikes, but he realizes it is wise not to let on what it is[3] - such as, "If we didn't need the new F-16s[4] I would have spilled water all over his pants."

The Secretary of State always bites his tongue so he won't blurt,[5] "The Premier is stubborn and obstinate and doesn't know up from down.[6] All he wants is war, and if he keeps doing what he's doing he's going to get one. Not only do I disagree with him diplomatically, I don't even like him as a person."

The Premier looks at the microphones and declares, "We are now going to have a friendly lunch." But what he says to himself is, "Inviting him to lunch was a mistake. He'll continue to talk and it will just give me another headache."

---

1) De Tocqueville :「토크빌의 저서」1985년 California 대학출판부에서 출판한 정치 사회에 관한 서간집. Charles Alexis Henri Clére de Tocqueville은 프랑스의 역사가, 정치학자. 19세기 전반(前半)의 정통 자유주의의 대표적 사상가.
2) not to be outdone :「상대방에게 지지않으려고」
3) not to let on what it is :「있는대로 말하지 않다」cf. let on =(slang) to pretend. to reveal a secret. Ex. *The imposter let on he was a company executive. Don't let on that I am ill.*
4) F-16s :「F16 (화이팅 햇콘) 전투기들」
5) blurt [blə́:t] : 엉겁결에 말해버리다. v. to utter abruptly or tactlessly. Ex: *blurted it out.*
6) doesn't know up from down =knows nothing.

5. Phi Beta[1] Money*

Word from the old alma mater is that the cost of private education is going up faster than the national debt. A recent College Board[2] survey revealed that the price of a diploma at one of the more expensive schools is now $75,000, which does not include gas, oil or ski trips during the school break.

Can parents afford to send a kid to college for $75,000 and still find happiness? The answer is, most people can't afford to send them for half of that. And yet for some reason the older generatio continues to do it. Thanks to their own sacrifice, parents are making their nut[3] and their children are growing up in the rich academic environment everyone has told them they are entitled to.

In order to get a better picture of what exactly is going on I talked to some of those involved in the tuition struggle[4] to see how they feel about it.

One student at Georgetown University took the news calmly. "Nobody wants to force our parents to come up with seventy-five thousand big ones, but if that's what we young Americans gave to pat for a good education, I say it's money well spent. Dad had it easy[5] when he went to college so he never knew the cost of a diploma. Now he's learning the hard way,[6] and he'll be better for it."

The drama concerning heavy tuition is being played out everywhere. I saw a father at Johns Hopkins[7] say farewell to his son at the gate. As he bade him

---

* 오늘날 미국의 명문사립대학 Harvard나 Yale을 졸업하는데에는 약 75,000불이 든다. 학부모들이 학비조달에 많은 부담을 느끼는 반면, 대학측은 그 정도의 수업료는 좋은 교육에 충분하지 못하다고 한다.

1) Phi Beta [fài bèitə] 희랍어 $\phi\ \beta$ =academic.
2) College Board : 「대학이사회」
3) nut : 「총비용」
4) the tuition struggle : 등록금 (학비) 염출을 위한 노력.
5) had it easy : 「편안한 경우에 있었다」
6) the hard way : 「고생하면서」
7) Johns Hopkins =The Johns Hopkins University.

goodbye, the father gave the young man his cuff links[1], tie clasp[2] and gold watch. "This is it,"[3] the father told the boy. "When they are gone you're on your own."

"Where will I find you?" the boy wanted to know.

"Your mother and I will be in the basement of a federal housing project[4] in Baltimore. Don't worry, the move has nothing to do with your tuition. We always planned to do it that way."

A president of one of the Ivy League[5] schools defended the high - priced costs and said that $75,000 barely pays for books and a half - baked[6] - history teacher.

"It's wrong," he explained, "to use the figure seventy -five thousand dollars as the cost of a four - year education, because now eveybody will expect one for that. We have a different plan at our school. We insist that parents throw everything they have into our rotunda[7] and allow the school to take what it needs."

"That sounds like a fair way of doing it," I agreed.

"Parents think we make money on tuition costing seventy - five thousand dollars. There is no way we can get in the black[8] by filling our classrooms," the president said. "We don't even make a profit on Shakespeare."

"What do you make money on?" I asked.

"Towing students' cars away. If it weren't for our police towaway program we would never have been able to construct a new science building."

The final person I spoke to was a football player attending a great Texas university.

"How do you feel about a seventy - five - thousand - dollar college education?"

---

1) cuff links : 커프스 단추
2) tie clasp : 넥타이 핀.
3) This is it : 「이것이 전부다」
4) a federal housing project (저소득자를 위한) 연방정부에서 건축한 공영주택.
5) Ivy League : 「아이비 리그」 동부의 유명한 대학 Harvard, Yale, Princeton, Colombia, Brown, Cornell, Pennsylvania, Dartmonth 등의 대학.
6) half-baked : 「미숙한」
7) rotunda [routʌ́ndə] : 「원형건물」
8) in the black : 「흑자로: 이득을 남기며」

He replied, "I don't think that's a lot of money to pay a linebacker.[1)] After all, we have given up a great deal[2)] to play football for our school."

"I believe you misunderstood me. The student is expected to pay the school, not the other way around."[3)]

"Why would a college football player want to pay the school anything?" he asked.

"Perhaps to get a better education."

"I'd rather see the seventy-five thousand go into new shoulder pads, where it belongs."

---

1) linebacker : (미식축구) 라인맨 바로뒤에 위치하는 수비하는 선수 n. a football player who is positioned just behind the line on defense.
2) given up a great deal 〈 give up a great deal : 막대한 희생을 하다.
3) the other way around : 역으로

6. She Does Nothing*

The worst thing you can ask a woman these days is, "What do you do?"

I made this mistake the other night when I turned to the lady seated next to me at a dinner party and posed the question.

"I don't do anythig," she said." I make breakfast for the family and then I clean the kitchen. After that I call the telephone company to find out if they plan on sending anyone to fix the phone, and then I go to the supermarket with a long list of things that we're out of."

"But you're doing something," I disagreed.

"I'm really not worth much," she sighed. "After the supermarket, I pick up my youngest child from kindergarten, and leave him at the baby-sitter while I go off in search of fertilizer for the lawn. I don't wear nice suits, and I never carry a briefcase."[1)]

"Look, if you don't want to talk about it, it's okay with me."

"I feel so worthless," she continued. "Sometimes when I want to have fun I go to the shoemaker and get new heels put on my shoes. But then I have to make up for it by taking the car to the garage[2)] because the brakes squeal, and the electrical system keeps dying on me.[3)] I've risen as high as I can in life."

"You do more than most women who work outside the home," I assured her.

"It's not true. Those women are suing people and figuring out celebrities' income taxes; they're removing gallstones[4)] and merging peanut companies with coal mine

---

* 가정에서 주부(主婦)의 일은 끝이 없다. 아무리 완벽하게 집안일을 한다해도, 밖에서만 활약하는 여성(女性)과는 비교 될 수가 없다.

1) I don't wear ~ a briefcase : 직업을 가진 사람들이 고가의 좋은 옷을 입고 가방을 들고 활약한다는 사실을 생각하면서 주부는 말한다.

2) garage : (주유소에 있는) 「자동차 수리소」

3) on me : 「나에게 난처하게도」 Ex. He died on me.

4) gallstones : 「담석」

monopolies. All I'm doing with my time is carting overdue books back to the library, driving my mother to the dentist, and trying to find a sump pump[1] for my basement. I'm almost ashamed to be in this room with so many women of accomplishment."[2]

"You're being too hard on yourself. Let's change the subject. What do you think of this lamb?"

"I never eat lamb. Nobody in my family likes it. But they do enjoy beef stew and it only takes me three hours to cook the whole thing. I love to be in the kitchen. No one has ever taken me out to lunch just because they wanted to sell me a new pension plan."

I must have touched a nerve somewhere because she wouldn't stop.

"Did I tell you I also compact garbage?"

"No, you didn't."

"What I do is taken the garbage,[3] put it into the machine and push a button, and then it gets compacted into a bag. But that's not all. When I've crushed enough garbage, I have to take it out of the compactor and insert a new bag. Now do you know what I do?"

"I'm very impressed," I answered.

"It's not as hard as it sounds, especially for those of us who went to Radcliffe.[4] What else would you like to know about me?"

"Do you have any dreams?"

"I dream of a big strong man coming to my house and saying, 'I am from the University of Virginia[5] Tau Omega fraternity[6] and part of my hazing[7] assignment is

---

1) sump pomp : 「배수펌프」
2) of accomplishment : 「공적이 있는; 성공한」
3) is take the garbage =is to take the garbage.
4) Radcliffe =Radcliffe College. Harvard 대학과 견줄만한 명문 여자대학 (현재는 남녀 공학).
5) University of Virginia : 돈 많고 오래된 가문의 출신들은 들어가기 쉽다는 말이 있다.
6) Tau Omega [tɔ:oumi:gə] fraternity. [TΩ] 친우회. Fraternity 남자학생 사교 구락부 cf. "Sorority" 비밀 입회식, 의식들이 있다.
7) hazing : 「신입생을 못살게 구는」〈 haze =to harrass and subject to humiliation (college freshmen, fraternity initiates, etc.)

to wash all your windows and bathe your dog,' I know it's too much to hope for, but I needed something to keep me going."

"Have you seen the Gauguin[1] exhibit at the National Gallery?"[2] I asked.

"I've been meaning to go but I have to wallpaper the kids' room, wait for the piano tuner to turn up, hem my daughter's dress, and buy a wedding gift for my niece, as well as make popcorn for my husband and his friends when they come over to watch the baseball playoff game."

"I don't understand why you keep putting yourself down[3]. You do quite a bit[4] for somebody who officially does nothing," I said.

"It's so little compared to[5] that woman over there who is giving my husband her business card."

---

1) Gauguin [gougǽŋ] : 「고갱」. 프랑스의 후기인상파 화가 (1848~1903). 타히티섬에서 죽다. (Euguste Henri Paul)
2) The National Gallery : 「국립미술관」
3) putting yourself down 〈 put one(self) down :「겸손하게 행동하다. 비하하다」
4) quite a bit : 「상당히. 많이」
5) compared to 〈 compare to =(미국) compare with.

7. No Smoking*

The firing squad[1] from Rikers Island[2] marched out onto the parade ground. Six soldiers, led by Captain Loughboro,[3] lined up at attention,[4] facing the wooden post.

Two soldiers, one on each side, marched Tony the Termite[5] to the post and tied his hands behind his back. Captain Loughboro stepped forward with a blindfold and tied it around Tony's eyes. "Would you care for a cigarette?" the captain asked.

"Yes, I would," Tony replied. "I'll take a king - sized mentholated."

The captain drew one out of a pack and placed it in Tony's mouth. He was about to light it when a uniformed inspector from the city's Anti - Somking Unit[6] ran onto the parade ground and cried, "Halt! You cannot smoke on this property during a firing -squad execution."

"That's ridiculous," the captain exclaimed. "Puffing a last cigarette before being shot is an ancient military tradition."

"Never mind tradition. No one is permitted to blow smoke within ten feet of another person as it's hazardous to everyone's health. Tony isn't doing harm only to himself but to the firing squad as well."

"Suppose I move the squad ten feet back?" the captain suggested.

"That still would be considered secondhand smoke.[7] Don't you have any respect

---

* 사형집행을 기다리는 사형수가 죽기전에 마지막으로 담배를 한대 피려고 했다. 그 사형수 앞에 금연단체의 일원이 나타나, 담배를 피면 구금30일과 50불의 벌금이라고 말한다. 사형과 범칙금, 어떤 쪽이 현명한 선택인가?

1) firing squad : 「총살대」
2) Rikers Island : 「라이카즈 아일랜드」 Manhattan과 Queens구와의 사이에 있는 East River에 있는 조그만 섬. New York시의 형무소가 있다.
3) Lough boro [lʌ́kbərou] : 라크보로.
4) at attention : 「차려자세로」
5) Tony the Termite : 백개미 토니. 사형수의 이름. cf. *Richard the Lion Hearted*.
6) Anti-Smoking Unit : 「금연단체명」
7) secondhand smoke : 「간접흡연」

for human life at all?"

The captain turned to Tony. "Would it bother you to give up your last cigarette?"

"It certainly would.[1] This is a free country and having one last puff is my right."

The captain riffled[2] through a book. "He's correct," he said to the inspector. "It says here no one may be shot unless he is offered a last cigarette of his choice."

"But we're only doing this for his health. If Tony sucks on that fag[3] he's going to develop a terrible cough."

"I'll worry about that," Tony protested. "It's too late to quit smoking. I should have done it years ago[4] when it had some meaning. Now let's knock off[5] the sweet talk and give me a light."

The inspector said, "That's the trouble with people who face capital punishment.[6] They think of nobody but themselves. We'll never have clean air if smokers ignore the rights of others. Well, I'm warning you. If the captain lights up your cigarette I'm going to arrest you for violating the law and it will cost you."

Tony asked, "What will I get?"

"Thirty days and a fifty - dollar fine."

"I'll take it. That's better than what they are going to give me now," Tony declared.

The captain barked at the inspector, "I won't hear of[7] it. This man has been sentenced to die by the firing squad and you are interfering in the outcome. Get out of here."

"I'm giving you notice," the inspector admonished, "that you can be locked up for

---

1) It certainly would = It certainly would. (bother me to give up my last cigarette)
2) riffled = to turn (pages) in quick succession, to leaf through quickly, *riffled through the book*.
3) fag (vulgar) = cigarette.
4) years ago = many years ago.
5) knock off = stop.
6) capital punishment = death penalty. Ex. *capital* offense.
cf. a *capital* error. Do not confuse *capital* with *capital*.
7) hear of : 「승인하다. 들어주다」
8) abettig 〈 abet = to encourage or assist in committing an offense.

aiding and abetting[8] a smoker, which is a capital crime. I suggest you dispense[1] with the cigarette and get on with[2] the execution."

Tony shouted, "I protest! No one can prove that smoking is hazardous to my health. I will fight to my dying breath to be able to enjoy this last cigarette because I have only one puff to give for my country. I say, 'Give me liberty or give me a Marlboro.'"

The captain snarled at the inspector, "Now you've done it.[3] We're not going to be able to shoot him until he goes to Smoke Enders."[4]

---

1) I suggest you dispense ~ = I suggest you (should) dispense ~
2) get on with ~ : 「~을 진행하다」
3) Now you've done it : 「자, 자네는 서투른 짓을 했네」
4) Smoke Enders : 「금연의 방법을 가르치는 단체명」

8. *Up in Arms' [1)]

Every night on the television you see people shooting at each other with everything from naval guns[2)] to rubber bullets. The screen is full of tanks smashing through villages and tear gas wafting on campuses. Whether it is the streets of Beirut or Northern Ireland,[3)] the entire world now appears to be an armed camp.

Nobody ever takes the time to ask, "Where is all this stuff coming from?"

The big surprise is not that it is so easy to buy equipment to start a insurrection, but rather that the people in sales don't even know whom they're selling the arms to.

Feaster, an arms merchant prince, said, "I love this crazy business. You never run out of surprises."

"What kind of surprises?" I asked.

"Look at this newspaper. The Israelis[4)] are helping the Chinese develop a new and improved Silkworm missile. As soon as it is tested, the Chinese are going to sell it to Saudi Arabia, and the Saudis will probably use if against the Israelis."

"Do the Israelis know this?" I gasped.

"Sure, but that's what makes the arms business so much fun. Take Iran.[5)] The country is the enemy of everyone in the world, and at the same time everybody's best arms customer. So what are they doing right now? The Iranians are buying weapons from France to sink ships belonging to the Western alliance, which France

---

* 무기상이 전세계에서 활약한다. 겉으로는 평화를 외치면서 말이다. 가장 큰 고객은 적국(敵國)일 수도 있고, 테러리스트일 수도 있다. 그들은 어떠한 거래도 모두 평화를 위한 것이라고 주장한다.

1) up in arms : 「전투준비를 하고」

2) naval guns : 「해군용 대포, 함포」

3) Beirut or Northern Ireland : 「두곳다 정치적 불안이 심하고 테러활동이 성행하는 곳」

4) The israelis [izréiliz] : 「이스라엘인」

5) Take Iran = Take Iran for example.

supports. Meanwhile, France is selling missiles to Iraq to sink Iranian ships."

"I guess you could lose your mind[1)] if you tried to keep track of whose side anyone is on in the armaments business."

"The Iraqis used the missiles they bought from France to hit a U.S. Navy ship despite the fact that the U.S. is helping Iraq in its war with Iran."

"I expect terrorists are big customers of arms dealers."

"The best. And they're getting bigger all the time. For a while they just bought the stray case of machine guns[2)] here, and a gross of hand grenades[3)] there. But now they're really upgrading their material and ordering designer weapons.[4)] As a result they have to be treated with respect."

"Do you impose any restrictions on what you sell terrorists?"

"No, but we ask them to try and avoid using the stuff in their own country. There is nothing wrong with selling bazookas to the Japanese Red Brigads[5)] to shoot down planes in Rome, while the Italian terrorists blow up an air terminal in Tokyo. It is what is known as terrorist reciprocation."

"Every country seems to be selling arms to the people it considers its enemies."

"That's what makes the business profitable for us. The reason weapons are so plentiful is that when we have orders from both sides, we can provide them so much more cheaply. Take Lebanon for example. There isn't a group in the entire country that won't buy everything we can supply. Every car bomb in Beirut has our name on it."

"And you don't feel guilty that you are paying a samll part in fanning the flames of war?"

"No. We're for peace. The other day a man from Lebanon came into the strore and wanted dynamite, detonators[6)] and a Volkswagen to blow up the headquarters of

---

1) lose your mind 〈 lose one's mind :「머리가 돌다」
2) the stray case of machine guns : 「바닥에 떨어져있는 기관총 상자」
3) hand grenades : 「수류탄」
4) designer weapons : 「부란드 물품(무기)」
5) Red Brigade : 「적색여단, 이테리의 테러리스트 집단」
6) detonators : 기폭장치, 뇌관.

a medieval church. As I was wrapping the package, I happened to mention that that particular faction had purchased one thousand mortars[1] just the day before. He thanked me and bought a tank to knock out their mortars. If I hadn't brought this up, someone in Beirut might have gotten hurt. So we do a lot of good in this business. Unfortunately, no one ever hears about it, mainly because arms dealers prefer to keep their good deeds to themselves."[2]

---

1) mortars :「박격포」
2) keep~to themselves 〈 keep ~ to oneself :「~를 사람들에게 비밀로 하다」

9. He's Out to Lunch*

So many readers ask, "What do people in Washington do all day long?" Believe it or not, we are no different from superachievers[1] in other parts of the country.

Most of the time we make telephone calls, leave messages and then wait for someone to return them. We measure our importance by how long it takes for a person to get back[2] to us.

Because of this, many Washingtonians have become experts on the smokescreen messages[3] the secretaries are sending out when we call.

Here's one that is heard frequently. I phone and give my name. I am put on hold[4], there is a pause of about forty - five seconds and then the secretary returns and says, "He's not at his desk right now." This makes me wonder. How far is her desk from the boss's desk for the secretary to take forty - five seconds to discover he is not there. Once in a while, when I lose my temper, I say, "Well, if he's not at his desk would you look and see if he is hanging outside the window?"

Many of the people I telephone are "in a meeting." Sometimes I want to know what kind of meeting so I ask, "Is it a Cabinet[5] meeting, an executive meeting, or a bowling team meeting?"

"What difference does it make?"

---

* 수신자가 부재시에 송신자는 주로 녹음으로 메시지를 남기는데, 워싱턴에서는 메시지를 받는 사람이 얼마나 빨리 전화를 건 사람에게 응답하는지가 상대방의 중요성을 평가하는 척도처럼 인식된다.

1) Superachievers : 「대성취자, 대성공자」

2) to get lack : 「(부재중에 전화를 받지 못해서) 녹음이나 비서의 message를 받아본 후 에 전화를 걸다, 회답전화를 걸다」

3) the smokescreen messages 있으면서 없는 척하며 하는 꾸민 말. 즉, *He's out to lunch; The Boss is in a meeting* : 또는 *He's in its court.*

4) am put on hold 〈 be put on hold : 「(전화로) 기다리게 지시받는다」

5) Cabinet : 「대통령 고문 위원회」

"I'd like to speak to him, and the only meeting I wouldn't want to interrupt is the one with the bowlng team."

The excuse that always bothers me is, "Mr. Dominick is tied up[1] at the moment." An image immediately comes to mind of Dominick tied to a chair with a gag[2] over his mouth, listening to an IBM saleswoman trying to convince him to buy a new personal computer.

Another notorious excuse for not talking to me is, "Mr. Califano is out to lunch." What's wrong with this message is that my call is at nine-thirty in the morning.[3] So I ask the secretary to gave him get back[4] to me before dinner as I have a two o'clock dental appointment.

I have a terrible problem with being rejected on the phone. My fears run amok[5] when I call someone and he won't talk to me, although I am certain he's there. In my mind I not only see him shaking his head at his secretary, indicating "no,no," but I also see his face breaking into a wide grin[6] while he is doing it.

As the day goes on I keep imagining a large pile of pink slips[7] on Califano's desk, and the one with my name on it is at the bottom. The worst part is that if I have to wait more than a few hours for the call to be returned, I usually forget what I telephoned about in the first place.

The most painful blow of all is when one's children don't call back.

I leave a message on my daughter's answering machine and days go by, maybe weeks, until she telepnones.

"Why didn't you get back to me?" I ask.

"I only listened to my messages this morning."

"Suppose it had been important?"

---

1) is tied up =is very busy.
2) gag : 재갈, 입마개
3) at nine-thirty in the morning: 아침 9시 반에
4) to gave him get back : 「그가 회답전화를 하도록 하다」
5) run amok =run amuck =lose control.
6) breaking into a wide grin : 「만면에 웃음을 띄우다」
7) pink slips : (미국영어) 해고통지(들) cf. Pink money, pink knot.

"Why are you calling if it isn't important?"

In Washington, our livelihoods and our self -respect are hooked up to the phone. It is an instrument that can either bring much happiness or destroy a fragile ego overnight.

The only way to avoid letting the telephone call get you down[1] is to make a game of it. I keep score. If someone calls me back within the hour, I give myself ten points; four hours, six points; eight hours, three points. If a person doesn't retrun my call within twenty — four hours, I deduct fifteen points. At the end of the day I add it all up. If I have accumulated more points than I have lost, I figure I'm still someone in Washington who has to be reckoned with..[2]

1) get (you) down : 「실망시키다」
2) be reckoned with : 「중요시되다, 상대해주다」

10. Thumbsucker*

The Thumbsucker Report has just been released. Written by Dr. Alfred Thumbsucker, the report deals with the porblems that parents have communicating with their children, and the inability of those children to communicate with anyone.

"Most parents," he told me, "admit that thy didn't have much luck with child — rearing, but they all have the same defense: 'Look what we had to work with.'"

"In your report, what do you consider to be the main barrier between children and their parents?"

"Rock music," he replied. "When teenagers turned to the Grateful Dead[1] for all their needs, parents lost control over them. It is not generally known, but as soon as a child is born in the United States, the doctor inserts tiny Walkman speakers into the ears. The Walkman is activated[2] when the doctor spanks the baby and it remains on at full volume right through college."

"You're going to make the front pages[3] with that one."

"As the child grows up, he or she spends evey waking moment listening to music, and tuning out on everything else. Parents were always under the impression that when a young person shook his head, he was answering either yes or no to a question. They had no idea that the kid was only keeping time[4] to the Rolling Stones."[5]

---

* 父子지간이나 母子지간에 의사소통(communication)의 단절이 심하다. 부모 자식간에 말이 통하지 않는 것은 아기가 태어날 때 의사가 갓난아기의 귓속에 워크맨의 스피커를 장치했기 때문이다.

1) the Grateful Dead 록음악의 밴드. 1965년에 결성되어 지금까지 활동을 계속하고 있다. 1987년에 발표된 "In the Dark"는 결성된 후 처음으로 hit chart Top 10 속에 포함 되었으며, 마이클 잭슨의 "Bad"를 앞질러 CD chart에서 1위를 기록했다.

2) activated 〈 activate : 「작동시키다. 시동시키다」

3) the front page : 「1면기사」

4) keeping time < keep time : 「박자를 맞추다」

5) The Rolling Stones : 「롤링스톤즈」 유명한 영국의 록그룹.

"Didn't it ever occur to a parent that something other than thinking was going on in[1] their offspring's head?" I asked.

"No, it didn't. Parents were happy to see their children snap their fingers because it meant that they were still alive. Some teenagers found that the audio level of the Walkman was not strong enough for their rock music habit, so they put large radios on their shoulders to enhance the sound. They also installed loudspeakers in their bedrooms so that nothing else could be heard in the house."

"With so much electronics at their command,[2] it's no wonder that kids have been unable to converse in any spoken tongue. This is the reason that parents never get a response when they shout, 'why don't you do what I tell you?' The child has no idea what his father or mother is saying."

"How can young people get by[3] without communicating?"

"Most of them have, discovered early in life that no matter what they did, they would always be housed and fed. Knowing this, there was no reason for them to try and figure out what was going on in the world."

"At least they know what they want," I said.

"The generations of rock music fans, all of whom are still wired with Walkmans, are now becoming the labor force in this country. They are doctors, lawyers and oil tanker captains, but they all keep time to Bruce Springsteen?"[4]

1) was going on =was happening.
2) at their command : 「그들이 자유로이 할 수 있는 마음대로 사용할 수 있는」
3) get by =manage to survive : 「(어떻게 해서든지) 지내다」
4) Bruce Springsteen : 1970년대 최후의 록가수. 밥 딜런의 영향을 받음.

"Did you interview a lot of people for your report?" I asked him.

"I talked to many parents, but they were more confused that helpful. The children were something else again. Every time I asked a question, they rolled their eyes and clapped their hands. I would have been worried had I not known[1] that each and every one of them had a Walkman implant."[2]

"Then your findings are based more on your own knowledge rather than on what anyone said to you?"

"That is correct. But it does have substance. I have never met a child who listened more to his parents than he did to Michael Jackson."

1) had I not known ~ = if I had not known.
2) implant : n.「체내에 심어넣는 것. 인프랜트」

11. Help Wanted*

Most commencement speakers lied to the graduating classes of 1987. They said that America wants them to become outstanding doctors, lawyers, nurses, dentists, scientists and college professors.

No one wants any such thing. What we really wish they could do is become[1] dishwashers, busboys, waitresses, taxi drivers, chambermaids[2] and gardeners.

Ebell Bowl, who gave the commencement speech at Luna Lake Tech,[3] was one of the thousands of speakers who admitted he made a mistake. We discussed it at a sidewalk café on Cape Cod,[4] waiting for coffee that never came.

"I should have told the class of 1987 that their generation owes it[5] to our generation to provide the basic services we all need[6] and I don't mean genetic engineering."[7]

"It doesn't count for a kid to climb the ladder of success if no one can get a cup of coffee," I said.

Ebell continued. "My message to the graduating class should have been that none of us can enjoy the American dream[8] if young people will not carry away our dirty dishes."

---

* 모든 사람이 학력이 높아져서 그 학력에 상응하는 직장에 취직하고, 또 높은 자리에 올라 간다해도, 서비스업에 종사하는 사람이 없다면 편리한 생활을 할 수 있을까?

1) is become =is to become.

2) chambermaids : 「(호텔이나 모텔에서 침대정리, 객실과 욕실의 청소를 하는) 청소부 아줌마」

3) Tech =Institute of Technology.

4) Cape Cod : 「케이프 코드」 Massachusetts 주 남동부에 있는 반도로서 고급휴양지.

5) it : 뒤에 나오는 "to provide the basic services"를 가르키는 가목적어 (假目的語, 형식 목적어)

6) we all need 앞에 있는 the basic Services를 수식하는 형용사절.

7) genetic engineering : 「유전(자)공학」

8) the American dream : 「미국의 꿈」 cf. *from ragsto riches.*

"I remember when I finished college how much I looked forward to being a bellhop[1] at a resort hotel. I couldn't have cared less[2] about upward mobility."[3]

Ebell became agitated. "I know what I should have said in my speech. This country will be great only when there are enough students to pump its gas."

"You could have made the point that since there are no illegal aliens[4] available, eveyone with an engineering diploma should pick grapes."[5]

Ebell said, "Higher education means bupkes[6] if there is no one to clean our hotel rooms. I don't want astronomers to tell me the world started with a bang. I want someone to explain why my air conditioner won't work. We don't need invstment bankers,[7] and marketing geniuses[8]– not as long as the country is crying for lifeguards and people to make Dunkin' Donuts."

"Why is there such a shortage of help?" I asked Ebell.

"Nobody will work," he replied. "The trouble is that kids don't think six dollars per hour is a fair wage for jerking sodas,[9] particularly since they can get twice as much from their parents if they promise not to drive sixty-five miles an hour."

Ebell added, "Attitudes have changed in recent years. At one time the greatest thrill[10] in the world for a young person was to wait on his friends in a restaurant. Now the biggest kick for a college student is to be waited on.[11] What's happened is that both the haves and have – nots want somebody else to do their menial work The haves wnat it all; the have– nots want it now. But nobody wants to work for

---

1) bellhop =n. a bellboy.
2) *couldn't have cared less.*
3) upward mobility :「출세 : 상승지향」
4) illegal aliens [eiljəns] :「불법입국자」
5) pick grapes : 포도송이를 따다.
6) bupkes [bʌpkəs] =이디슈어. (slang) beans, nothing, very little.
7) investment bankers :「투자금융업자」
8) marketing geniuses :「시장분석 전문가들」
9) jerking sodas 〈 jerk sodas : 훼스트 푸드(편의점)점에서 탄산음료를 용기에다 레버를 사용하여 넣다.
10) thrill =kick (쾌감)
11) to be waited on :「서비스를 받는 것」

tips."

"If eveyone is sitting down, who will mix our malted milkshakes?"

"I made a lot of mistakes at the graduation. I shouldn't have told the students their job is to stop a nuclear holocaust.[1] I shoud have assured them that the most they can do for peace is clean fish[2] so people won't go hungry in South ampton."[3]

"Even if you had said it, they wouldn't have listened."

Ebell continued. "Not one of those youngsters has a fight to demand a piece of the American pie[4] if he or she hasn't paid his dues to Wendy's.[5] This country can't survive if its graduates insist on bypassing the summer jobs that go begging."[6]

"Had you mentioned that in[7] your talk, you would have received a standing ovation[8] – from the parents."

"Not only that" said Ebell. "We might also have been served our coffee."

---

1) a nuclear holocaust. : 원자폭탄으로 인한 대학설
2) is clean fish =is to clean fish 생선의 내장을 떼내다.
3) South ampton [sauθ æmptən] : Long Island 남쪽연안에 있는 부자 사람들을 위한 고급 여름 휴양지.
4) American pie : 「(누구나 모두 구하지만 일하지 않으면 얻을 수 없는) 미국의 꿈」
5) Wendy's : 「웬디즈」 유명한 햄버거 점
6) go begging (신청하는 사람이 없어) 제발 일해달라고 부탁하다.
7) Had you mantioned that~, = if you had mentioned that~
8) a standing ovation : 「청중들의 기립 박수갈채」

PART Ⅲ

1. A Personal Message

By *James Reston*[1]

After 48 years as a reporter on *The New York Times*, writing a column two or three times a week for more than 30 years, I concluded a little while ago that a man can stick in the trench too long.[2]

It's not that writing a column is so hard. As my old buddy [3]Red Smith used to say, all you have to do is open a vein and bleed.[4] But if you have to do it on deadline,[5] you sleep funny the night before.

George Bernard Shaw[6] tried it for a few years on *The Spectator* in London but finally gave it up because, he said, he felt like a man standing under a windmill.

Just when he finished an article, he said, one sail of the windmill[7] would knock him over, and when he staggered through another column, the next sail would send him spinning... and the next and the next.

So I'm not moving out[8] but just moving over[9] out of the way to write when I please, confident despite the recent silliness in Washington that things here are seldom

---

1) James Reston : *New York Times*지의 편집국장, 부사장을 역임했다. 다음 글은 그의 고별칼럼전문이다.
2) can stick in the trench too long. : 「한 구덩이(직장)에 너무 오래 눌러 있었다.」
3) buddy : 「단짝, 동료」
4) open a vein and bleed : 「심정을 토로하다.」
5) on deadline : 「마감시간에 맞추어서」
6) George Bernard Shaw(1856~1950) : 「영국의 극작가」
7) one sail of the windmill : 「풍차의 날개」
8) move out : 「아주 떠나다」
9) move over : 「자리를 옮기다」

as good or as bad as most people think they are.[1)]

Officials are no worse today than they used to be, but the reporting is better. People know more about the danger of atomic weapons, so we haven′t had a world war for over 40 years whereas there were only 20 years between the two great catastrophes[2)] of the century.

In America, we have learned something about how to deal with adversity since the Great Depression,[3)] but not much about how to deal with prosperity. We're very rich but we′re not having a very good time. We are producing so much food that we don't know what to do with the garbage, while half the human race goes to bed hungry every night.

I have some other funny ideas. I think we′ve won the cold war and don′t know it. I think the Constitution is still working on its 200th birthday, against the corruption in politics, commerce and even in the pulpit.[4)] I don't like nuclear weapons or the plague of AIDS,[5)] but fear may be bringing us to our senses.[6)]

It takes a strong country to survive a Government that doesn't know what's going on in its own shop[7)] and sweeps the Persian Gulf without minesweepers,[8)] but things balance out. If this no-fault Government[9)] the people chose not once but twice were any better we wouldn't deserve it, and if it were any worse, we couldn't bear it.

Even so, we're probably going to get an agreement with the Russians to eliminate all short-and medium-range nuclear weapons, the first real reduction in these monsters since the invention of the atom bomb.When we do, both sides will still be left

---

1) things here are seldom as good or as bad as most people think they are : 「세상 돌아가는 일은 많은 사람들이 생각하는 것 만큼 좋지도 않고 나쁘지도 않다」
2) two great catastrophes : 「1, 2차 세계대전」
3) Great Depression : 「세계대공황」
4) the pulpit : 「종교계」
5) AIDS : 「후천성 면역 결핍증」(*a*cquired *i*mmune *d*eficiency *s*yndrome)
6) bringing us to our senses : 「정신을 차리게 하다」
7) its own shop : 「일터」여기서는 정부 사무실.
8) minesweeper : 「소해정(掃海艇)」
9) no-fault Government : 「최근의 잇단 실정에도 불구하고 레이건 자신의 인기 덕분으로 고비를 넘기고 있는 현 행정부를 가리킨다.」

with more than twice the number of nuclear weapons they had at the time of the Cuban missile crisis, but we're turning a corner.[1)]

All the nations are speaking in different voices about the ideal goal of human life. In the Golden age[2)] of their dreams, "nation shall no more lift sword against nation...,"[3)] the free development of each will lead to the free development of all.... "the world shall be full of the knowledge of the glory of the Lord, as the waters cover the sea."[4)] But with regard to the roads to this ideal, there is utter confusion and the clash of contradictory opinion acted upon with the violence of fanaticism. There is, however,a gleam of hope.

For all the nations, including our own, are discovering the limits of ideology. President Mitterrand is modifying[5)] his Socialism in France, Mr. Reagan is looking at his deficits[6)] and wondering about his"supply-siders,"[7)] and even Mikhail Gorbachev is recognizing that Communism, on the 70th anniversary of the 1917 Revolution, has been a spectacular[8)]economic and philosophic failure.

So after more than 50 years in journalism's greatest era - a quarter of the two centuries since the pamphleteers[9)] wrote the Constitution — I remain an up-to date,[10)] stick-in-the-mud[11)] optimist.

There are theaters[12)] of violence, rebellions and uprisings of all sorts, mass hypocrisy and false sincerity fueled[13)] by television, and a general decline in courtesy

---

1) turn a corner : 「고비를 넘기다」
2) the Golden age : 「황금시대, 전성기」
3) nation shall no more lift sword against nation." : 「*the Old Testament*의 Isiah의 2 : 4의 일부분」
4) the world shall be full of the knowledge of the glory of the Lord, as the waters cover the sea : 「*the Old Testament*의 *Habakkuk* 2 : 14」
5) modifying : 「수정하다」
6) deficits : 「(재정, 국제수지)적자」
7) supply-siders : 「(레이건 경제정책의 기초를 이루는)공급측면 경제론자들」
8) spectacular : 「엄청난」
9) pamphleteers : 「18세기 미국의 정치논설은 주로 pamphlet형식으로 발표되었다」
10) up-to-date : 「현대적인」
11) stick-in-the-mud : 「고루한, 시대에 뒤진」
12) theaters : 「현장」
13) fueled : 「부채질 하는」

and a decay of decency; but I don't despair.

I would feel better if marriage were more popular, but I doubt if so many people were ever so well fed, well read[1] or bright-minded and curious and critical as the rising generation is today.

A while ago, I gatheread some of these old columns in a book that my old sidekick[2] Alastair Cooke reviewed in *The New Yorker.* When I thanked him for his amiable lies,[3] every one of which I enjoyed, he explained that there were only two kinds of obituaries — vertical and horizontal,[4] and he thought I'd like the vertical sort better.

So I'm off[5] for a while, and I have some plans for what's left of my vertical years. I'm going to slow down my backswing.[6] I'm going to move my vegetable garden at Fiery Run closer to the kitchen door, and I'm going to spend a little more time on Martha's Vineyard[7] before they hang out the standing-room-only signs.[8] Later, I'm going to try to bring back the smoke-filled room[9] so that the next Presidential candidates will be chosen by people who know something about them. And finally, if I'm lucky, I'm going to write a long love letter to America.

---

1) be well read :「많이 읽는, 박식한」
2) sidekick :「동료」
3) amiable lies :「애교있는 거짓말」
4) obituaries-vertical and horizontal :「수직적인 부고(訃告)와 수평적인 부고. 여기선 산 사람(vertical)에 관한 것과 좋은 사람(horizontal)에 관한 글 이라는 뜻」
5) I´m off :「떠난다」
6) I´m going to slow down my backswing :「좀 느긋하게 살련다」
7) Martha´s Vineyard :「Massachusetts주의 Cape Cod의 남쪽의 섬. 휴양지」
8) standing-room-only signs :「(극장 같은데서)입석 외 만원 표지판」
9) smoke-filled room :「요인들의 비밀회의실」

2. Just Feels Like The Age of Change

By *Keith Kachtick*

I turned[1] 26 a couple of months ago. The occasion seemed less a cause for celebration than a reason[2] to renegotiate my contact with the future. My life has become a compromise. Expectations made in youth have been postponed, standards set for adulthood have been forgotten or ignored. Certainly I am no longer a child, but neither am I at a point that I can consider myself a full-fledged[3] adult : I still wear baseball caps, still order beer with dinner,[4] still keep *Playboy* face down in the sock drawer.[5] I am both proud of and embarrassed by the fact that I own neither a credit card nor any type of health insurance. And though I'm beginning to actually enjoy Mozart and Bach and all the others, I still don't have the slightest interest in knowing anything about them.

Twenty-six seems to me the very middle of life's first holding pattern,[6] a foggy gray area between becoming and being.[7] I took off at 21 and presumably will land around the age of 30. I'm in no hurry, but sometimes I worry how far there is to go.

---

1) turn : 「나이 ~살을 넘기다」
2) less A than B : 「A라기보다는 B이다」
3) full-fledged : 「어엿한」
4) order beer with dinner : 「보통은 와인을 저녁식사와 함께 주문하다」
5) keep *Playboy* face down in the sock drawer : 「양말장 안에 플레이보이 잡지를 겉표지가 밑으로 가게 감춰둔다」
6) life's first holding pattern : 「인생의 첫번째 대기경로」 holding pattern은 항공기의 착륙 차례를 기다리는 선회이다.
7) becoming and being : 「생성과 존재」

At 26, Picasso had completed his blue period.[1] What should I be doing at this point in my life? What should I have already done? Should I be raising kids or my expectations? Should I even be asking questions like these?

My friend Alex, a waiter / freelance photographer,[2] has been 27 for almost six months. He doesn't like it. "I' m beginning to look like my father," he complains. "I act like him, I talk like him, I even smell like him." The implications of this make me nervous. " My friend George, a bartender/freelance playwright,[3] recently turned 25. He says, "When I look in the mirror now, I find myself thinking: If I were a tree, all my life would be in the leaves."[4] He didn't use to talk like that.

I have heard my grandfather say that his 20's were the worst years of his life. "Between 20 and 30, he explained to me, nodding like a man who lived to tell about it, that a fellow is too young to know better and too old to care.[5] Yet my father claims that if he could go back in time, he would stop right where I am now. "You're at the peak of your life," he argues," and at the peak you can see squarely[6] where you've been and squarely where you're going." Maybe so. Either way, the view is unsettling.[7]

Probably it's true that we all want the excitement of a new life as well as the guarantee that nothing will ever change— the desire[8] to fly without risking a fall. But it's also true that genuine changes are irreversible, once we've jumped from the plane we can't climb back in. The way I see it,[9] life is a series of these changes: minor ones

---

1) the blue period : 「피카소(1881~1973)의 청색시대(1901~1904)」. 그 다음이 the rose period(1905~1906)이다.
2) freelance photographer : 「전속이 없는 자유 사진 작가」
3) playwright : 「극작가」
4) all my life would be in the leaves : 「나의 생활은 나뭇잎처럼 민감하고 불안정할 거야」
5) too young to know better and too old to care : 「뭘 잘 알기에는 너무나 젊고, 걱정하기에는 너무 철든」
6) see squarely : 「직시하다」
7) the view is unsettling : 「그런 견해는 마음을 불편하게 한다」
8) guarantee : the desire는 the excitement, the guarantee와 동격
9) the way I see it : 「내가 인생을 보는 바로는」

can occur every six months or so, and may lead to self-knowledge; major ones, I'm told, come once or twice a lifetime, and often lead to nervous breakdowns[1] or the writing of books.

The first clue that I'd hit the era of the Major Change[2] was the realization that I've become preoccupied with other people's ages. I'm now asking every one how old he is, even complete strangers. ″ Hi. My name's Keith. I'm 26. How old are you? ″ I don't recall doing this as a teen-ager, and I certainly don't see many of my older friends (I know they're older because I've asked) harassing one another this way. Suddenly, age has become my life's barometer. At 26, I'm gauging my readiness[3] to jump by the success and failures of others. It doesn't matter whether they're jumping into marriage, their first salaried job, a new city, or a new way of parting their hair.[4] 26 just feels like the age of change — and I believe I'm now old enough to expect the worst.

Philosophically, I'm more ontological.[5] Questions that I ignored in college are now genuine concerns. Why am I here? What is absolute? How can somthing be infinite and not be infinity? And there are certain things I wasn't expecting to feel at this age, but do: I now take pride in my hometown (Austin, Tex.). I'm convinced that travel is more important than graduate school. I believe what goes around comes around,[6] and that some day my landlord will drown in shallow water.[7] I take seriously the challenge to consider everything,[8] dismiss nothing. And I've come to trust that there is a purpose to life, that somewhere someone much wiser than I is keeping an eye on what's happening, and that in the big scheme of thing[9] what I do and don't do

1) nervous breakdown : 「신경쇠약」
2) that I′d hit the era of the Major Change : 「내가 전화기에 도달했다는」
3) gauging my readiness : 「나의 준비상태를 재다」
4) parting their hair : 「머리 가리마를 타는」
5) more ontological : 「더 존재론적이다」
6) what goes around comes around : 「간 만큼 되돌아 온다」
7) drown in shallow water : 「(재수가 없으면)얕은 물에서도 빠져 죽을지 모른다」
8) take seriously the challenge to consider everything : 「모든 것을 샅샅이 고려하라는 제안을 따른다」
9) in the big scheme of things : 「만물의 거대한 체계하에서」

somehow matter.[1)]

The day after I turned 26, my father called to wish me a happy birthday. During our conversation, he offered some unsolicited advice[2)] about this or that, which I summarily refused to consider. "Dad," I said sharply, "try to remember that I am an adult." There was a long silence. The hollowness of my words seemed to echo through the receiver. I am an adult. Right. Real drinkers don't count their beers, real adults don't declare their realness.

As I hung up, I looked at myself in the mirror. Adulthood, I realized, is self-evident. You simply recognize it when you see it. Right now, I see only this: At 26, I'm more of a man than I think I am,[3)] and I'm more of a boy than I think I should be. I'm old enough to feel tired of myself, but still young enough — thank God! — to believe in the possibility of change.

---

1) matter : 「문제가 되다」
2) unsolicited advice : 「청하지 않은 충고」
3) I'm more of a man than I think I am : 「내가 생각하고 있는 것 보다 나자신이 더 어른스럽다」

3. The Isolated Scientist

By *Ronald N. Kahn*

I always secretly hope that people won't ask me what I do. When I tell them I'm a physicist, conversation stops. My life as a scientist, in fact, is a life of isolation. Nonscientists seem to have no interst in learning much more about me or my work. Other scientists, the ones who best understand what I do, are not much help. Often, they are my closest competitors.[1)]

Is this a man's problem? I think so. Women in science, because there are so few, face their own special problems. Moreover, the scientific world I live in is one of fierce competition, merit based on achievement,[2)] disdain for outsiders, the classic man's world.[3)] The isolation I feel as a scientist is a consequence of living in a male-dominated world. In this regard, all men are scientists.

But all men do not have the social problems we scientists share. When nonscientists meet me and learn my occupation, they seem immediately to bring into play[4)] a strong set of assumptions and stereotypes[5)] about scientists. They assume that I'm brilliant but incomprehensible. They place me in a separate world, a ″higher″ world perhaps, one beyond theirs. They assume that there are no links connecting their world to mine. They are convinced scientists care only about science and are possessed

1) my closest competitors : 「가장 가까운 경쟁자」
2) merit based on achievement : 「연구업적에 근거한 평가」
3) the classic man′s world : 「전형적인 남성세계」
4) bring into play : 「작동하다」
5) assumptions and stereotypes : 「억측과 상투적 편견」

by it[1] — look at Frankenstein,[2] look at Dr. Strangelove.[3] Scientists, they assume, care nothing for the lives and interest of ordinary people.

Although I have some ambivalence about[4] this reaction — I enjoy being viewed as brilliant — I don't really want to live in a separate world. I don't feel like a mad scientist. I enjoy literature and art, talking about politics and the law. I want to understand all of the world, mine as well as nonscientists.

Nonscientists also generally assume that they have nothing to say about my work that would interest me. I don't see it that way . Most scientists, in all fields of specialization, care about how their work relates to the general human condition. This is the source of their motivation.[5] And in my own work, I concentrate on questions that are philosophically interesting[6] — deciphering[7] the very early history of the universe. This field consists of many small tasks, and my daily routine involves struggling with mathematical details and searching for breakthroughs[8] usually so tiny that only I can appreciate them. The drudgery,[9] though, is in service to[10] broad questions of general interest, and I wish I could, more often, share some of the ideas my work raises. I am fortunate to have a wife with whom I can share interests. She contributes to my thoughts about science and I try to understand her writings on social theory.

It would seem to me that everyone would have something — religious or philosophical — to say about the origins of the universe. In fact I've found that everyone does have

---

1) possessed by it : 「과학에 들린」
2) Frankenstein : 「자기를 파멸시키는 힘을 만들어 내는 사람」 영국의 작가 Mary Wollstonecraft Shelley(1797~1851)의 소설의 주인공.
3) Dr. Strangelove : 영화 *Strangelove*(1964년)의 주인공. 군국주의자이며 광신적인 전략가로 대규모 핵전쟁을 주장한다.
4) have some ambivalence about : 「~에 관해서 상반된 감정을 갖고 있다」
5) the source of their motivation : 과학자들에게 동기를 부여하는 힘.
6) philosophically interesting : 「원리적인 입장에서 관심을 끄는」
7) decipher : 「해독(판독)하다」
8) breakthroughs : 「(발견에 의한)비약적인 전진」
9) drudgery : 「단조롭고 고된 일」
10) in service to : 「~을 위하여」

one cosmology[1)] question to ask me. Unfortunately, it's always the same question. (Will the universe last forever?) That wouldn't bother me, except that I usually feel it's just a desperate attempt to find something to say.

My reaction to belonging to a separate culture is generally to cover up the fact.[2)] I avoid mentioning my occupation. (I began this sort of behavior as an undergraduate, when I would say that I attended college in New Jersey rather than reveal that I went to Princeton.)[3)] I talk about nonscience topics. But to do this exclusively is to live out a lie.[4)] Science clearly represents a major part of my life. When my true colors[5)] are revealed, I do try to explain the importance of my work, but usually with little real success. Everyone starts by agreeing with me, then eyes glaze over[6)] and the conversation ends. Maybe it's my fault.

But perhaps science and the arts, the two cultures described by C. P. Snow,[7)] really are widely separate. Perhaps I should never expect true understanding outside my own realm. Perhaps I should stick to the world of scientists.

Clearly, all scientists understand the life of others of their kind.[8)] Perhaps none understand exactly my day-to-day scientific struggles, but I do share interests with a small group of people and a common world view with a much larger set.[9)] Occasionally this leads to true feelings of camaraderie.[10)] In graduate school I felt the bond of common adversity[11)] — students versus the system and the established

---

1) cosmology : 「우주론」
2) cover up the fact : 「그 사실을 감추다」
3) I attended college "in New Jersey" rather than reveal that I went to Princeton : Princeton대학은 New Jersey주의 Princeton에 있기 때문에 이렇게 말했다.(I attended college in New Haven하면 Yale대학을 뜻한다).
4) live out a lie : 「본심과는 반대로 행동하다」
5) my true colors : 「나의 정체, 본색」
6) eyes glaze over : 「눈들이 흐리멍텅해진다」
7) C.P.Snow(1905~1980) : 영국의 소설가, 과학자. he Two Cultures and the Scientific Revolution(1959)라는 강연에서 문학도와 과학자 간의 간격을 논하였다.
8) others of their kind : 「여러 분야에 있는 다른 과학자들」
9) a much larger set : 「더 많은 사람들」 a set=a group
10) camaraderie : 「동지애」
11) the bond of common adversity : 「공통의 역경을 겪음으로써 맺어지는 유대」

professors; students simultaneously tacking a vast bulk of knowledge, developing a way of seeing the world. We felt a bond because we had chosen the most difficult academic path.[1] We sometimes felt that we were better than nonscientists.

I have seen other forms of scientific camaraderie, but always in this mold of us – against-them, our-group-versus-theirs rushing to publish first,[2] to achieve fame and glory.

Even camaraderie like this is rare. Scientists, as opposed to nonscientists,[3] do not assume other scientists are brilliant. They assume that they are stupid (though still smarter than nonscientists). Worth is measured in intelligence as defined by achievement,[4] and everyone is struggling to advance. And so it turns out that many of those who understand me best are my adversaries. Scientists are isolated from nonscientists and also from one another.

Where does this leave me ?[5] I am not optimistic about any decline of competition in the near future. In fact I see some advantages to competition;[6] things do get done. (I am, as you can see, a product of the system.)[7] The undesirable side effect, the emotional isolation, will remain.

I am more hopeful about closing the gap between the two cultures. Technology is assuming an ever-increasing role in modern life, forcing scientists and nonscientists closer together. For my own part, I'm determined to try harder to show the accessibility of science, to teach nonscientists new scientific questions, and to demonstrate a new view of science — science as art, perhaps, or at least science more obviously connected to everyone's world.

---

1) the most difficult academic path : 「가장 힘든 전공」
2) rushing to publish first : 「남보다 먼저 발표하기 위해 서두르며」
3) as opposed to nonscientists : 「비과학자들과는 대조적으로」
4) as defined by achievement : 「학적 업적에 의해 평가되는」
5) where does this leave me? : 「그렇다면 어떻게 될 것인가?」
6) advantages to competition : 「경쟁의 이점」
7) a product of the system : 「체제의 산물」

4. Made In U.S.A

By *Peter Vail and Alexander Genis*

Two absolutely incommensurate events led us to ponder the state of affairs in contemporary America. The first was the tragic loss of the Challenger space shuttle,[1] an event known to the entire world, and the second — the purchase of some bookshelves by one of the two authors of this essay.

The tragedy in space was a painful blow to the entire nation. America, at the very peak of its prosperity, was seen by many as having lost face.[2] It was an accident which placed in doubt[3] the very essence of this prosperity. It may appear obscene to compare this national tragedy with petty, everyday difficulties, but we found a common factor linking the cosmic accident with what we experienced in making a very ordinary purchase.

It started when we decided to buy some bookshelves. Like many others, we decided to order directly form the factory. We chose a design, the material, the lacquer color, made a down payment,[4] and agreed on a delivery date.

When that day arrived, everything was prepared. The books had been removed from the old shelves and were strewn in untidy heaps on the floor. Delivery time came and went, but nothing happened. We were overcome with a desire to complain, demand blood,[5] truth, an explanation. But our English was not up to the task,[1] nor was

1) space shuttle : 「우주 왕복선」
2) having lost face : 「체면을 잃었다」
3) placed in doubt ~ : 「~을 의심하게 했다」
4) down payment : 「계약금 또는 월부구입의 첫 불익금」
5) demand blood : 「(피의 대가로)피를 요구하다」

our knowledge of the American way of life.

Two weeks passed, the various piles of books began to be covered with dust and mildew,[2) and family members shouted themselves hoarse with irritation.[3) Finally the delivery men arrived. The first thing they did was collect the remainder[4) owed for the shelves. Then they carried in the pieces from which the bookshelves were to be assembled. A glance at the unpacked boards was enough to convince anyone that they were more fit for a coffin than for bookshelves. None of them seemed to be the same size. All the components of what was ultimately to be transformed into furniture[5) differed in height, width, depth, and virtually any other characteristics you could name.

This sad saga could be continued,[6) but it is sufficient to say that after 12 telephone conversations, in which a number of people participated — including one United Nations interpreter — the bookshelves were partly abandoned to the despair of the garbage can.[7) Still, the scene of our story lends an extra spiciness to it.[8) After all,[9) this happened in Manhattan, and not some provincial city such as Voronezh.[10)

We lent a sympathetic ear to other victims of[11) the American economic system. We learned that, aside from bad moods and premature grayness,[12) the low quality of American goods has had enormous social and economic consequences — among

---

1) our English ~ to the task : 「영어실력이 짧아 그렇게 하지 못하였다」
2) mildew : 「곰팡이」
3) shouted ~ with irritation : 「짜증이 나서 목이 쉬도록 큰 소리를 쳤다」
4) collect the remainder : 「잔액을 받다」
5) what was ~ furniture : 「끼어 맞추다 보니 가구(책장)모양이 드러난 것」
6) this sad ~ continued : 「이런 슬픈 이야기는 하자면 끝이 없겠다」
7) abandoned ~ the garbage can : 「절망한 나머지 쓰레기통에 던지고 말았다.」
8) the scene ~ lends an extra spiciness to it : 「우리 이야기의 장소 탓으로 놀라움이 가일층 더해진다」
9) after all : 「요컨대」
10) Voronezh : Don강 유역의 소련의 지방도시
11) lent a sympathetic ear to other victims of : 「동정심을 가지고 다른 피해자들의 이야기를 경청했다」
12) aside from bad moods and premature grayness : 「언짢은 기분과 조급한 비관은 차치하더라도」

them our own unpleasant experience in purchasing furniture, the Challenger accident, the mushrooming trade deficit, and a general decline in the prestige of the "Made in U.S.A label.

Do you remember that cherished label ?[1] Do you remember the tremulous bliss[2] that overcame all of us when we saw those modest initials, whether we were from Moscow, Odessa, or Riga?[3] No matter where we read them — on a shirt, a chewing gum wrapper, a fountain pen, or a pair of sunglasses — for us this label was a true mark of quality. And it had to do with more than any single consumer item,[4] it signified a quality of life, the quality of an economic-social order. To be blunt,[5] it signified the quality of the capitalist system of production.

By the middle of the '70s, the proud captains of American industry[6] were resorting to a humiliating appeal:"Buy American!" That is, buy items with the "Made in U.S. A" label, not because they are of higher quality, but because they are made on home turf.[7]

But Americans are too practical to permit patriotism to interfere with the family budget.[8] They may purchase a flag decorated with stars and stripes,[9] but their television is "Made in Japan." And how can you blame them if a Japanese TV is far more reliable than its American competitor?

Automobile manufacturing is particularly humiliating. If any one object symbolizes the proud "American way of life", it is the car. The automobile has made the

---

1) that cherished label : 「그렇게도 소중하던 상표」
2) the tremulous bliss : 「짜릿한 행복(감)」
3) Moscow, Odessa, or Riga : 소련의 도시이름들.
4) it had to do with more than any single consumer item : 「그것은 어느 한 가지 상품에 국한된 것이 아니었다」
5) To be blunt : 「솔직히 말하자면」
6) the proud captains of American industry : 「미국산업계의 당당한 지도자들」captains of industry은 20세기 초 미국산업의 급속한 진보를 주도한 인물들을 지칭.
7) on home turf : 「본 고장에서」
8) are too practical to permit patriotism to interfere with the family budget : 「워낙 실용적이어서 생활비를 지출하는 데 애국심 따위를 고려하지 않는다」
9) a flag decorated with stars and stripes : 「성조기」

country.[1] It is not simply a means of transportation, but part and parcel of the very soul of the nation.[2] And after all this[3] ungrateful Americans will get into any car other than one built in America. There's no getting around the fact that[4] Americans prefer anything not built in America. There now exists a psychology of mistrust for domestically produced items.

This mistrust is strengthend by catastrophes such as that of the Challenger. We remember all too well that three of the eight helicopters sent to rescue the hostages in Iran broke down almost immediately. The ordinary consumer has the right to assume that if even specially selected military technology is unreliable, what can he expect of his toaster or stereo system?[5] When the next tragedy occurs, this consumer will grieve together with his nation, but he will view the "Made in U. S. A. label with a still more jaundiced eye.[6]

Today America is desperately striving to comprehend how the United States lost its economic prestige. Some sociologists see the explanation in technology. Why, they reason, do we pay extra[7] for items bearing a "hand-made" label ?[8] Because the assembly-line process degrades quality.

The technological revolution is itself to blame for[9] the failures of the American economic system. Like any revolution, it corrupts people. As one example, the inno-cent hand-held calculator[10] has deprived people of the ability to count. You go to the store and the salesperson needs the register to add 10 and 10.

We believe that the decline in the prestige of American goods, as well as all the

---

1) defines the lifestyle of the country : 「이 나라의 생활양식을 특징 짓다」
2) part and parcel of the very soul of the nation : 「이 나라의 정수」
3) after all this : 「이 모든 것에도 불구하고」
4) There's no getting around the fact that : 「~한 사실을 부인할 수 없다」
5) what can he expect of his toaster or stereo system : 「토스터나 전축을 믿을 수 있을까?」
6) with a still more jaundiced eye : 「더욱 편견에 찬 눈으로」
7) pay extra=pay more money.
8) items bearing a "hand ~ made" label : 「"수공품"이라는 상표가 붙은 물건」
9) is itself to blame for : 「~의 책임이다」
10) the innocent hand-held calculator : 「손에 들고 있는 아무렇지도 않은 계산기」

other catastrophes such as aviation losses and our own vain expectations of book shelves, can be explained by a decline in the American ethic.

Hermann Hesse in his 1943 Nobel Prize-winning utopian novel *The Glass Bead Game* had this to say about the collapse of Western Civilization:.

> It soon became clear that the intellectual spinelessness[1)] and low moral level of several generations might be sufficient to cause real harm to everyday life and that in technology and all important areas, skill and a sense of responsibility are encountered more and more infrequently... People either know or vaguely sense that if thought becomes muddied and sluggish, then respect for spiritual and intellectual integrity will be weakened.

A total idealist, Hesse believed that a strong army or a healthy economy is less important for the survival of humanity than the creation of a spiritual - intellectual aristocracy capable of devoting a lifetime to writing a dissertation on " the Latin pronunciation of institutions of higher learning[2)] in Southern Italy in the late XII century."

The American dream[3)] seems to have no room for the intellectual side of life.[4)] There is prosperity, freedom, and justice. The Founding Fathers[5)] believed that a person possessing these virtues would automatically become an intellectual who would read Horace[6)] in the original.

They were wrong. America has no time for Horace. The average American family watches television something like eight hours a day. Eight! One third of the time is spent sleeping, one third working, and one third watching TV.

---

1) the intellectual spinelessness : 「정신력(용기)이 없는 것」
2) institutions of higher learning : 「대학」
3) The American dream : 민주주의, 평등 자유 등 미국 건국의 이상과 물질적인 번영과 성공이라는 미국의 꿈.
4) have no room for the intellectual side of life : 「지적 추구와는 관계가 없다」
5) The Founding Fathers : 「미국건국의 부조」
6) Horace[hɔ́rəs] : 고대 로마의 시인.

Of late, art in the United States has taken on[1) a more popular nature, become more primitive, more tawdry. Film critics complain that Hollywood is lowering quality in direct proportion to quantity. Last year *Amadeus* won the Oscar; it was made by Milos Forman, a Czech. But the viewers preferred *Rambo, Police Academy*, and Spielberg films, which are pleasant but absolutely mindless.[2)]

American mass culture has created an extremely unattractive image of the American. The entire world is now troubled by the spread of bad taste[3)] associated with the "Made in U.S.A" label. The French are demanding that American slang be removed from their word stock,[4)] and the Italians are protesting against the opening of a McDonald's[5)] in Rome. Even the backward Third World is trying to hold back[6)] the flood of American serials[7)] on the television screen. Throughout the world (with the possible exception of the Socialist countries) "American"has become a synonym of bad taste.

We realize that our view of America is tendentious[8)] and biased. This country has many fine museums, orchestras, and publishing houses. Most of the Nobel Prizes from Stockholm end up here.[9)] America has a refined and even esoteric[10)] culture at many levels.

Nevertheless, every time we turn on the television, every time we hear of a plane crash, every time we buy a hot dog, when we see lines of people waiting to get into *Star Wars*, everytime we see the latest list of best sellers, we recall what that gloomy idealist Herman Hesse said about the role of intellectual culture in the cheerless year 1943.

---

1) take on : 「(성질, 특성 따위를)띠다」
2) mindless : 「속이 없는, 어리석은」
3) bad taste : 「조잡한 취미」
4) work stock : 「언어」
5) a McDonald's : 「McDonald Hamburger연쇄점」
6) hold back : 「저지하다」
7) American serials : 「미국의 TV연속 프로그램」
8) tendentious : 「의도적인」
9) end up here : 이곳(미국)으로 오고만다.
10) esoteric : 「비전(秘傳)의, 심오한」

5. A Publisher Reflects on Freedom of the Press

By *Tom Johnson*
(Publisher of the Los Angeles Times)

As a publisher, I am acutely aware of the many disputes between the media and their critics. Some of this criticism is deserved;[1)] some is not. Criticism of the press is as old as the press itself. A free press that does its job is bound to irritate segments of society.[2)] The peril we face is that some of these critics attempt to translate their irritation into action that would limit our rights. We see this threat in ever-increasing libel judgements[3)] around the country and in continuing efforts to restrict press access to judicial proceedings[4)] and to government information.

We have earned some of this response through occasional lapses in editorial judgement,[5)] and our occasional failure to meet reasonable standards of accuracy and fairness has led many to suspect the press's own ethical commitments. Not long ago the *Los Angeles Times* conducted a national poll on the public's perception of the press. Nearly 40 percent of the respondents said they think that the mass communications industry misuses its great power by acting irresponsibly. Nearly 20 percent said that abuses[6)] by the media should be dealt with more sternly by government regulators. Only

---

1) is deserved : 「그러할만한 가치가 있다」
2) segments of society : 「사회의 일부 계층」
3) libel judgements : 「명예훼손 판결」
4) judicial proceedings : 「소송절차」
5) lapses in editorial judgement : 「논설의 판단을 내리는 데 있어서의 실수」
6) abuses : 「남용」

one in four thought the media to be essentially ethical : one in three said we are fair in our handling of the news.

Such perceptions suggest that a considerable segment of the public sees the press as an artful dodger[1] — darting out from the sanctuary of shield laws[2] and the First Amendment,[3] using our powers over public opinion to do mischief , and then darting back to shelter to escape retaliation. Such a characterization is unfair and inaccurate, and it misrepresents the reasons for the Constitution's protection. But it is not entirely unexpected: the argument that people resent the bearer of bad news has considerable merit, and the news is by no means always good. The press is the institution we love to hate,[4] and its role as public watchdog and advocate is not likely to make it consistently popular.

The press has its weakness, and these must be acknowledged. We seek excellence, but no institution can rid itself of all imperfection. There indeed have been violations of journalistic ethics. Because the transgressions of one reflect poorly on all,[5] each violation sounds an alarm throughout the profession. Instead of offering excuses or retreating behind the well-worn rhetoric of[6] the people's right to know, we must always have the courage to recognize our errors and the wisdom to seek ways to correct them. Increasingly, I think, some newspapers are beginning to do that. Newspapers operate in an ethical climate wholly different from — and more demanding than --- the climate of just a generation ago, and I find that encouraging.

Our critics seem to forget that it is from the press itself that they learn about our transgressions. When *Washington Post* reporter Janet Cooke was found to have fabricated a story about an eight-year-old heroin addict, it was *The Washington Post* that

1) artful dodger : 「요리조리 잘 빠져나가는 교활한 사람」
2) shield laws : 「방패가 되는 법률」
3) the First Amendment : 「미국 헌법의 The Bill of Rights의 제 1조로서 신앙.언론. 집회의 자유를 제정한 것」
4) love to hate : 「규탄하기를 좋아하는」
5) the transgressions of one reflect poorly on all : 「한 신문의 위반은 모든 신문에 좋지 않은 영향을 미친다」
6) the well-worn rhetoric of : 「~라는 진부한 미사여구」

carried the most detailed story on what had happened. When the Securities and Exchange Commission[1] began investigating charges that a *Wall Street Journal* reporter who wrote a market column had leaked information to Wall Street brokers before publication[2] it was *The Wall Street Journal* that published a long, detailed story about the case on its front page. Nor are such remedial actions[3] confined to the press. In response to criticism that network vote projections[4] have unfairly influenced elections, *ABC News* recently decided to refrain from predicting the outcome of races[5] until the polls have closed in each state being analyzed.

We need no new laws, executive orders, or restrictive court decisions to regulate the press. That would be odious, unconstitutional, and inimical to[6] the best interest of our democratic way of life. Nor do I think such mechanisms as ombudsmen[7] or news councils can or should replace the judgment of publishers, editors, and reporters.

The fact remains that some members of our profession have been guilty of conflicts of interest or of presenting fact as fiction or of irresponsible or prejudicial reporting or of other kinds of improper or unethical behavior. There are fewer of these incidents today than in the past, but their repercussions are felt throughout our profession.[8] These are serious violations of the trust vested in our free press by the public and by our constitutional system.

The press can do little to allay the suspicions and hostilities of those in government, business, or elsewhere in our society who have an ax to grind against it.[9] But we

---

1) the Securities and Exchange Commission : 「증권거래위원회」
2) before publication : 「활자화되어 공표되기도 전에」
3) remedial actions : 「시정방안」
4) network vote projections : 「(방송국의)투표결과 예상 방송」
5) the outcome of races : 「선거결과」
6) inimical to : 「저해하는」
7) ombudsmen : 「(시민의 권리를 지키는)민원 조사관」 여성형은 ombudswomen.
8) their repercussions are felt throughout our profession : 「그 영향은 언론계 전역에 파급된다」
9) have an ax to grind against it : 「딴 속셈이 있는」여기서는 언론을 벼르고 있는.

should — we must — try to ameliorate[1)] the legitimate resentments that many others have toward us. Those resentments will persist until we are consistently willing to apply to ourselves the same standards we demand of others. We cannot demand access to the councils of government, to the courts, and to corporate board - rooms,[2)] and then turn away[3)] critical writers who come to our own doors with potentially embarrassing questions. Nor can we demand answers of those we interview and then say "no comment" or we stand by our story when we ourselves are challenged.[4)] In short, we cannot insist on accountability[5)] from other powerful institutions in our society while simultaneously rejecting accountability for ourselves.

We are entirely correct, and we fulfill our constitutional obligation, when we expose folly, untruthfulness, and conflicts of interest in government or when we challenge secrecy in the judicial system. The press can demonstrate how corporate decisions[6)] may spawn[7)] new problems or have unforeseen (and sometimes destructive) consequences. That is the role the Constitution guaranteed to a free press.

Unfortunately, good intentions and practies do not guarantee success. Even if we are consistently candid about our shortcomings, and as forthright[8)] as we expect others to be, a skeptical segment of the public is likely to continue to consider us just another powerful institution, enjoying the unfair advantage that comes with our unique constitutional protection.

But a responsible press will serve the public interest, not private privilege ; as long as our ethical principles place primary emphasis on that end, we will annoy as regularly as we will satisfy,[9)] and assaults on our rights and credibility will assuredly

---

1) ameliorate : 「개선하다」
2) boardrooms : 「이사(중역)회의실」
3) turn away : 「퇴짜놓다」
4) when we ourselves are challenged : 「우리들이 답변을 요구받았을 때」
5) accountability : 「책임」(=responsibility)
6) corporate decisions : 「기업체의 의사결정」
7) spawn : 「이야기하다」(알을 낳다)
8) forthright : 「솔직한」
9) annoy as regularly as we will satisfy : 「(언론은)대중을 만족시키는 만큼이나 대중을 귀찮게 하기도 한다」

continue.

I believe that most of the people — the ultimate beneficiaries[1] of a free press — continue to look to us as a guarantor of their liberty. This support demonstrates a fundamental public confidence in our ability and determination to do our job, and do it well, within our constitutional framework. This is a source of satisfaction. It should not be an invitation to complacency.[2]

If Congress shall make no law abridging the freedom of the press, the public must expect us to maintain standards worthy of that freedom. I believe that, by the measures on which we judge any institution in our society, the press has done so.[3] Because we are exposed to public scrutiny[4] every day, we have a particular responsibility to meet those ethical standards we have set for ourselves. Freedom is hard won and easily lost. Trust and fairness are the values to which a free society must demand devotion. We know what those standards ought to be, and it is the continuing responsibility of the press to strengthen our collective resolve to adhere to them.

---

1) the ultimate beneficiaries : 「궁극적인 수혜자」
2) an invitation to complacency : 「자기만족에로의 유인」
3) the press has done so : 「언론은 언론의 자유를 받을 만한 기준을 지켜왔다」
4) we are exposed to public scrutiny : 「대중이 언론을 예의 주시하고 있다」

6. A Book Can Transform a Life

By *Allan Bloom*

When I was 16 years old, I left my home in Indianapolis to enroll[1] at the University of Chicago. Robert Hutchins,[2] the president of the school, was not a great scholar. But he had tremendous enthusiasm for the idea of a liberally educated man.[3] An excitement about reason filled the university. And the curriculum,[4] built around the Great Books,[5] was rooted in the belief that there are universal ideas men could study that would show the oneness of human life.

I started out by reading Marx,[6] Freud[7] and Weber[8] ; all of whom I'd only heard about in high school. Marx told us how to get rid of the evils of the oppressive bourgeois system. Freud spoke of our repressed desires. Weber revealed value relativism to us. It all seemed to be adult and exciting. It was as if I had discovered that life, instead of being a harmonica, was a great organ with hundreds of stops.[9]

In my early years at the university, Plato and Aristotle were background figures.[10] We were told that they were important, but the Greek way just did not seem to be

---

1) enroll : 「입학하다」
2) Robert Hutchins(1899~1977). 미국의 교육자. Chicago대학 총장.
3) a liberally educated man : 「신사가 될 교양교육을 받은 사람」
4) curriculum : 「교과과정」
5) Great Books : 「고전」
6) Marx, Karl(1818~1883) : 독일의 사회주의자.
7) Freud, Sigmund(1856~1939) : 오스트리아의 의사. 정신분석학 창시자.
8) Weber, Max(1864~1920) : 독일의 사회학자. 정치경제학자.
9) stops : 「pipe organ의 음관열, 음전」(=stop knob)
10) background figures : 「배경인물」

our way. We read them because we had to. But capitalism, the unconscious and the id[1] seemed to be what really mattered. Marx, Freud and Weber seemed newest and truest. I remember Aristotle saying that the philosophic life is the highest life, and I thought to myself : " Well, a dentist would say that dentistry is the highest life. "

But, gradually, I discovered philosophy. When I read Plato's *Republic* and came across the parable of the cave,[2] that was a magic moment. I was overwhelmed by the idea that humans live in a cave looking at shadows on the wall which contain a little reflection of the truth and that education represents turning from the shadows to the source of light. Plato said we don't know the sources of all things, but we know somethings. That made wonderful sense to me, as did Pascal's[3] magnificent phrase: "We know too much to be skeptics and we know too little to be dogmatists."

When I was 19 and beginning graduate school at Chicago, I met the man who was to be my mentor,[4] Leo Strauss. At the time, I still believed that Aristotle and Plato were essentially limited by their economic and historical situations. I thought that all truths changed with historical epochs — that because most people in the fifth century B. C. believed in the Greek gods that Plato, too, must have. Strauss asked me: "Why do you think that?" I couldn't answer. I had been so certain that there was no access to the truth, that we were children of our culture[5] and our time. But Strauss made a good case for[6] Plato talking beyond the ages, seeing all that we see and perhaps more. I became convinced that just because there are many different cultures, that doesn't mean there is no transcultural truth.[7] The study of philosophy was incumbent on[8] all of us, I thought — the need to explain ourselves is

---

1) id : 「(정신분석학)개인의 본능적 충동」
2) the parable of the cave : 「동굴의 비유담」다음 문장에 그 설명이 나온다.
3) Pascal, Blaise(1623~62) : 프랑스의 철학자, 수학자, 물리학자.
4) mentor[méntoːr] : 「스승, 선생」
5) children of our culture : 「우리 문화의 소산(산물)」
6) made a good case for~ : 「~을 옹호하다」
7) transcultural truth : 「각 문화를 초월하는 진리」
8) incumbent on~ : ~에게 지워지는 의무이다. (It is incumbent on you to advise him. 그에게 충고해주는 것이 당신의 의무이다)

irrepressible.

Students of mine have had similar transforming experiences. A book or an idea has opened new vistas[1] for them. When I was teaching at Yale, I had a student named Thomas Pangle who wanted to be a lawyer. One day in class, I gave a little speech about Socrates. Until then, Pangle wasn't very interested in philosophy. But when he heard me speak of the need to compare the legal order to the just order, that connected with him,[2] he became preoccupied with the problem of justice and spent years on it as a philosophy professor at the University of Toronto. I have had lapsed[3] Catholic students who read Dante's *Inferno* and suddenly found that their religion was not something they could just dismiss. It became a theme of a lifetime. A student at Cornell read John Locke,[4] and as a consequence the question of what was the moral content of America beyond the selfish desire for gain became a tremendous issue for him.

There are an infinite number of starting places to begin one's quest for the truth. Reading Plutarch[5] can be a thrill for those with great ambition. Others have erotic motivations and start with Plato's *Symposium*, or Freud. The modes of touching a student are diverse. But there can be for many a moment of revelation[6]— a book or an idea that serves as an intellectual launching pad.[7] Plato led me to Rousseau, Nietzsche and others. *The Republic* was the foundation. Then came Rousseau, the great egalitarian critic[8] of Plato who, in some sense, imitated him: He wanted to have a democratic equivalent of the Republic. Nietzsche spoke in the name of human greatness against the leveling he believed Rousseau had made epidemic.[9]

---

1) vista : 「(정신적)전망」
2) connected with him : 「그의 관심을 일깨웠다」
3) lapsed : 「신앙을 버린」
4) John Lock(1632~1704) : 영국의 경험주의 철학자
5) Plutarch(46?~120? A.D) : 희랍의 사가. 전기작가
6) a moment of revelation : 「계시의 순간」(=epiphany)
7) launching pad : 「발사대. 출발점」
8) egalitarian critic : 「평등주의 입장에서의 비판가」
9) make epidemic : 「퍼뜨리다. 유행시키다」

Each writer contains pointers[1] to others. Nietzsche, for example, wants something like religion, but thinks the Bible is no longer viable. Anybody who is serious about the Nietzschean experience then has to check the Bible to see whether he is right.

One needn't set up a canon of[2] books to read. In fact, I think such lists are rather silly . The important thing is to find one book and follow where it leads. In that way, a whole world can be constructed that moves from philosophy to literature, art and music. If you touch the heart with one book, it can transform a life.

(Allan Bloom is a political philosopher who teaches at the University of Chicago and is author of the best seller *The Closing of the American Mind.*)

1) a pointer = a helpful hint or suggestion.
2) a canon of = a list of.

7. Liberal Arts In An Age Of Technology

By *Leland Miles*

Let me sketch in[1)] the value of the liberal arts as I see it : First, they enrich our minds ; second, they ennoble our character ; third, they expand our horizons; fourth, they increase our insight independently of[2)] what we do and are vocationally. The liberal arts pertain to us[3)] as human beings, to us as personalities, regardless of whether we are nurses, or engineers, or business executives, or whatever.

I don't mean to imply by this that the liberal arts have no practical career benefits. In fact, I have felt for some time that the humanities[4)] in particular make a mistake in not arguing on the enemy's ground.[5)] The enemy says, "We want practicality, " so I say, "Very well, the liberal arts are practical. How do you get ahead in a corporation or in any organization? You cannot get ahead without understanding how groups interact with each other chemically.[6)] You cannot get ahead without psychological insight. You cannot get ahead without imaginative passion. You certainly cannot get ahead without being able to communicate with people."

Those qualities constitute[1)] the art of human relationships. Those qualities

---

1)sketch in : 「상세히 설명하다」(=depict)
2)independently of~ : 「~와 관계 없이」(regardless of)
3)pertain to us : 「우리와 관련이 있다」
4)the humanities : 「(문학, 언어, 역사, 철학 등)인문학」
5)make a mistake in not arguing on the enemy's ground : 「반대자의 논거를 수용하지 않는 실수를 하다」
6)chemically : 「화합해서」(=in harmony)

constitute the art which the humanities, the social studies and fine arts can provide to those who study literature and philosophy and psychology. Also, liberal arts provide a moral framework within which sound decisions are made.

The fact remains[2] you cannot make sound decisions without some moral framework, and that[3] is particularly what the humanities provide. Corporations are begining to recognize this.

Another great value of the liberal arts is that they provide a source of stability in a period of incredible flux[4] and change. The book *Megatrends*[5] informs us that data will soon be doubling every 20 months. That means we will soon be, and already are, drowning in information. We are being drowned in information but simultaneously we are being starved for[6] knowledge.

Please note the difference between those two words. Many people use those two words synonymously. They are not synonymous. Computers give you information. The liberal arts give you knowledge. They give you the power of discrimination.[7] They give you some sort of scale of values[8] by which you can decide what's irrelevant or unimportant. We can then push the unimportant items into the round file[9] and concentrate on the relatively few important things that come across your desk[10] each day.

Megatrends also tells us that we are moving now at the speed of light[11] in our society. I read recently that we will soon have planes that can cross the Pacific (from the United States) in three hours.

---

1) constitute : 「이루다」(=make up)
2) The fact remains～=It is still a fact ～ remains ～ that
3) that : some moral framework
4) flux[flʌks] : 「끝없는 변화」
5) *Megatrends* : 미국의 미래학자 John Nisbitt 와 Patricia Aberdeen 공저(1982년).
6) starved for : 「굶주리다」
7) power of discrimination : 「식별력」
8) some sort of scale of values : 「어떤 종류의 가치기준(척도)」
9) round file : 「휴지통」
10) come across your desk : 「책상위에 놓여지는」
11) the speed of light : 「광속」

We now have telexes and radio telephones which can reach anyone anywhere, even on a freighter.[1] Moreover, we now have electronic letters[2] to allow you to do your business in an hour.

As a student said to me recently, "Man,[3] we are really moving." We are indeed moving, but where are we going? Where are we headed? What's the goal? Where is the time for reflection even to identify a goal? I think of Thoreau[4] who said, "He who runs the fastest need not carry the most important messages." And paraphrasing that, he who moves the fastest in our age does not necessarily have the wisest goal.

For me one of the greatest things that studying the humanities does is to give you stability. *Tess of the D'Urbervilles*[5] gives you stability. *Hamlet*[6] and "Ode on a Grecian Urn"[7] give you stability because they are classics, because they are universal and important forever, because they get better and better the more you read them and therefore give a sense of permanence in a world that is in perpetual flux.

There is one other aspect of the liberal arts that I want to mention, and that is something that will strike a responsive chord in many of you.[8] The liberal arts are valuable in emergencies.[9] I want to give you just one very dramatic example. Some of you might have read an article in *The Atlantic*[10] several years ago by a U. S. Navy Commander. He was graduated from the U. S. Naval Academy. His specialty[11]

---

1) freighter : 「화물선」
2) electronic letters : 「전자(컴퓨터) 글씨」
3) Man(감탄사) : 「정말」
4) Thoreau Henry David (1817~1862). 미국의 시인. 수필가. 숲속의 생활(*Walden* 1854)의 저자.
5) *Tess of the D'Urbervilles* : 영국의 작가Thomas Hardy(1840~1928)의 소설(1891).
6) *Hamlet* : William Shakespeare(1564~1616)의 비극(1603).
7) "Ode on a Grecian Urn" : 「희랍 항아리송(頌)?」영국의 시인 John Keats(1795~1821)의 시(1820).
8) strike a responsive chord in many of you : 「많은 독자의 공감을 불러 일으키다」
9) in emergencies : 「비상사태시에」
10) *The Atlantic* : 미국의 문예, 정치 종합 월간지(1857~).
11) specialty : 「전문, 전공」

was technology. He was a Wing Commander,[1] very much admired by his flying mates[2] for his skill and his technological expertise.[3] He flew in Vietnam and was shot down. He was in prison for four or five years and when he came out he told how he remained sane.

What he did every day in his small cell[4] was to take[5] some work of literature or philosophy that he had studied at the Naval Academy, and he concentrated on the work in his cell all day long. He took Plato's *Apology*, the dialogue in which Socrates is put on trial. And then he took Plato's dialogue *Crito* in which Socrates is offered escape but refuses to take it because he thinks as a citizen he should obey the law. He took Plato's *Phaedo*, in which Plato advances[6] the idea that you can't arrive at truth until you separate the soul from the body, that is until you die. Every day our naval officer concentrated on some classic, thinking through all its implications.[7] One day he took Beethoven, another day *Oedipus Rex*,[8] another day Michelangelo and the Sistine Chapel[9] paintings. Every day he got through[10] that day by meditating on great literature and art. When he came out of prison he wrote his article in *The Atlantic*. The article was really a paean of praise[11] for the liberal arts and what they meant to him as a person who was primarily a technologist.

It might well be that some of our personal tragedies haven't been that dramatic. But I would guess that for many people the liberal arts, in times of stress, have been a similar spiritual reservoir.

---

1) Wing Commander : 「비행단장」
2) flying mates : 「동료 비행사」
3) expertise[ekspʌə(:)ti:z] : 「전문지식」
4) small cell : 「(수용소의)독방」
5) take : 여기서는 contemplate, think의 뜻.
6) advances : 「개진하다」(=states)
7) implications : 「함축」
8) *Oedipus Rex* : 「오디푸스 왕」희랍의 Sophocles(496~406 B.C)의 비극.
9) Sistine Chapel : Vatican 궁전에 있는 교황의 성당.
10) get through : 「용케 넘기다. 보내다」
11) a paean[pi:ən] of praise : 「찬사의 노래」

8. Inaugural Address

By *Benno C. Schmidt.*[1)]

We carry forward the Puritan zeal for education as the path to salvation. The Puritans embodied the scholastic[2)] determination to rationalize faith and the conviction that learning showed the way to truth. In their radical[3)] dependence on the world of God lay a radical capacity for collective independence in matters of politics, a respect for mind, and an intensity of striving and spirit that are the hallmarks of great intellectual achievement. Observing the ineluctable[4)] progress of the Puritans' educational institutions toward liberality of thought and magnanimity of mind,[5)] we may even go so far as to[6)] suggest that in their radical dependence on the word[7)] lay the seeds of the heretical imperative,[8)] that irreductable[9)] individual obligation and freedom to which the Greek verb *hairein* refers — to choose — that is the essence of intellectual freedom.

From its beginnings Yale has been intimately of another community,[10)] also born

---

1) 1986년 9월20일 예일대학 개교 285주년의 총장(Benno C.Schmidt)취임사.
2) scholastic : 「학문적」
3) radical : 「철저한, 완전한」
4) ineluctable : 「피할 수 없는」
5) magnanimity of mind : 「도량이 큰 마음」
6) go so far as to : 「~까지도 ~하다」He went so far as to say that ~. 그는 ~라고 까지 말했다.
7) the word : 「성경의 말씀」
8) heretical imperative : 「이단적인 명제」
9) irreductable : 「축소될 수 없는」
10) another community=academic community : 「학계」

of Puritanism. I refer to the American community of higher education.

From its rudest beginnings Yale has not been an island in the community of higher education. The presence of so many honored guests[1] from great institutions around the world testifies to our deep sense of educational community. The central mission of the university is to preserve, disseminate, and advance knowledge through teaching and research.

The foundation of this mission is academic freedom and absolute adherence to freedom of expression within the university and the associated freedoms and protections that sustain it.[2]

In respect of[3] its commitment to academic freedom, as in all other respects, Yale is not a sanctuary apart from American society. It is rather an integral reflection of our society's commitment to pluralism, private ordering,[4] and institutional and personal autonomy in the pursuit of freedom of inquiry and expression.

No institution devoted to the spirit of free inquiry can survive in a society so riven with doubt and fear[5] that it hunkers down[6] in futile rejection of the ugly truths of our imperfect world, the complex vision of modern science, or nonconforming[7] ideologies and affiliations.

Intellectual freedom is hard pressed[8] in the United States today. Our officials in Washington exercise their discretion over[9] such matters as visits to the United States by foreigners thought to carry a controversial message or the degree of secrecy in matters thought to relate to that most umbrageous of concepts,[10] national security, with little thought for intellectual freedom. They seem to be under the

---

1) honored guests : 「귀빈」
2) it=freedom of expression within the university.
3) In respect of ~ : 「~에 관해서는」 =with regard to.
4) private ordering : 「개개인에 의한 우선 순위의 선택」 personal freedom
5) riven with doubt and fear : 「회의와 두려움으로 분열된」
6) hunkers down : 「움추리다」
7) nonconforming : 「비동조적인」
8) is hard pressed : 「압력을 받고 있다」
9) exercise their discretion over~ : 「~에 그들의 재량권을 행사하다」
10) that most umbrageous of concepts : 「가장 수상한 개념」

misimpression that they are the ideological nannies[1] of a population of preadolescents[2] rather than the servants of a free and responsible people. And I speak of both parties, and liberals and conservatives alike. Even more threatening is the insidious[3] tide of conformity and fear that menaces so many of our public schools, where offending books[4] are ransacked from libraries, science is subverted to sectarian ends,[5] and teachers are harassed[6] for intellectual convictions, elections[7] of private lifestyles, and simple commitments to truth. And even our great universities need not look back to the paranoid excesses of the McCarthy era[8] to find assaults on intellectual liberty. Speakers have been hounded and intimidated into silence by forces both inside and outside the unversity. Scientific investigation has been throttled[9] out of misplaced fears[10] and fantasies, and teachers and students mercilessly harassed for their research interests, their politics, their sexual identities.

We will protect our own with fierce resolve. But Yale is not an island where intellectual liberty is at stake[11] ; we must never ask for whom the bell tolls[12] when academic freedom is jeopardized.[13]

I think the principles developed for the governance of our civil society are not an adequate account of the place of freedom of expression at Yale. The theoretical roots of our Constitutional commitment to free expression lie in capacities for political

1) ideological nannies : 「이념의 보호자」
2) preadolescents : 「사춘기 이전의 어린이들」
3) insidious : 「음흉한」
4) offending books : 「국가시책이나 미풍양속에 배치되는 서적」
5) sectarian ends : 「분파적인 목적」
6) are harassed : 「시달리다」
7) elections : 「선택」
8) the McCarthy era : 1950년대 미 상원의원 Joseph Raymond McCarthy(1909~1957)가 위원장이 되어 반국가.용공주의자들을 무차별로 고발하여 물의를 빚었던 시대
9) throttled : 「억누르다」
10) misplaced fears : 「그릇된 두려움」
11) at stake : 「위험에 처하여」 My life is at stake 내 생명이 위험에 처해 있다.
12) for whom the bell tolls : 영국시인 John Donne(1571~1631)의 시 'Devotions upon Emergent Occasion'에 나오는 말. Hemingway의 소설 제목이기도 하다.
13) is jeopardized=is at stake.

participation and an abiding intellectual skepticism embodied in Justice Oliver Wendell Holmes, Jr.'s[1] view that truth is the shifting residue of competition in ideas.[2]

The problem with these theories of free expression for a university community is their failure to address[3] what freedom of mind is really about, which is, how to think. We need to confront expression not because it gives us information, permits us to participate in decision-making — although those are useful — but because we need to develop our own capacities for freedom. To stifle expression because it is obnoxious,[4] erroneous, embarrassing, not instrumental to some political or ideological end is — quite apart from the grotesque invasion of the rights of others — a disastrous reflection on ourselves.[5] It is to elevate our fear and our ignorance over our capacity for a liberated and humane mind.[6] It trammels our capacity for salvation over our fearful and parochial selves.[7]

The critic George Steiner,[8] among others, has been forcing our attention to the truth that a literate humanistic culture was certainly no barrier to totalitarianism. Not only not a barrier, but in certain instances, as Steiner wrote, the citadels[9] of culture and art welcomed the new barbarians. It is a matter of record that the faculties of some great universities offered little resistance to the degradations[10] that occurred inside — as well as outside — their walls.

The question Steiner is forcing us to contend with[11] — and it is profound, certainly disturbing and not easily answered — is whether there is something in the

---

1) Justice Oliver Wendell Holmes, Jr.'s (1841~1935)미국 법률가이자 대법원 판사. (1902 ~ 32)
2) the shifting residue of competition in ideas : 「사상의 경쟁에서 걸러지면서 살아남은 것」
3) address=consider.
4) obnoxious : 「불쾌한, 역겨운」
5) disastrous reflection on ourselves : 「우리들 자신의 비참한 처지를 반영하는 것」
6) humane mind : 「인간미가 있는 마음」
7) parochial selves : 「편협한 자아」
8) George Steiner(1929~) : 프랑스 태생의 미국의 문학 비평가.
9) citadels : 「보루」
10) degradations=degenerations. 「타락」
11) contend with : 「해답하다, 씨름하다」

very nature of the intellectual enterprise,[1] in its abstractness, in its[2] neutrality, in its remoteness from the texture and the exigencies of daily life, that diminishes our capacity for moral response.

I think not, and finally neither does Steiner.

There is a simple truth about liberal arts education and that is — that studying what is outside us is an open, curious, even playful way can give us two indispensable gifts. One is happiness. And the other is the gift of empathy.[3]

Liberal education should prepare us for a lifetime of such vulnerability and risk. Or as Eliot[4] put it in the *Four Quartets*,[5] a life in which "the pattern is new in every moment and every moment is a new and shocking valuation of all we have been." Our education in the end prepares us not only for our professions, but for the two-thirds of our life that is not about our jobs, our work, our status. But about dailyness. About inwardness. About our capacities for affiliation.

Finally I would like to end on a personal note, one that is inspired by a line in the *Four Quartets* that seems especially relevant as I stand here today. "We have had the experience but missed the meaning.

---

1) intellectual enterprise : 「지적활동(추구)」
2) its : of the intellectual enterprise.
3) empathy : 「공감, 감정이입」
4) Eliot, T.S.(1888~1965) : 미국 태생의 영국의 시인, 비평가.
5) *Four Quartets*(1944) : T.S. Eliot의 장시.

9. An Interview with Alvin Toffler

MODERATOR: In 1970, Alvin Toffler introduced a new concept: future shock. Noting accelerating technological change, Toffler questioned society's ability to adapt to the future. His books, *Future Shock* and *The Third Wave*, are required reading[1] in universities and corporate headquarters.[2] His latest book, *The Adaptive Corporation*, has continued his analysis of social change.

I would like to go now directly to our participants overseas to receive their questions.

Q : Mr. Toffler, please elaborate on[3] the proliferation[4] of nuclear military arms and minor powers.[5] I think that in the next 20 years there may be dangers for global security.

A : I think you are right. In the United States one of the terms used for the cowboy's six-gun[6] was "the great equalizer." It made even small and weak cowboys as strong as John Wayne. The dispersion of arms in the world has similar effects: quite small states can be armed with megaweaponry. Then the rest of the world has to sit up and take notice[7] if these states decide they want something.

I cannot believe that the present structure of world power, essentially bipolar, can

1) required reading : 「필독서」
2) corporate headquarters : 「회사의 수뇌진」
3) elaborate on : 「상세히 설명하다」
4) proliferation : 「확산」
5) minor powers : 「군소국가」
6) six-gun=six-shooter.「6연발 권총」
7) sit up and take notice : 「바짝 정신 차리다」

continue indefinitely in its present form — the alliances and the regional arrangements[1] made after World War II, when the economies of many European states were war ravaged and the United States and the Soviet Union emerged as the two dominant powers. I think we will move, whether quickly or more slowly, toward some sort of restructuring of the political arrangements in Europe; and that occurs at the same time that the Pacific region is becoming ever more important economically.

So, I think that 25 years from now the world geopolitical picture[2] will look quite different. Meanwhile, I do not believe that the United States and the Soviet Union will launch a nuclear holocaust; but I do not at all rule out[3] the possibility of "small wars" or possibly even "small nuclear wars."

Q : Please expound more on[4] the matter of the Challenger and Chernobyl disasters. It seems technology and economic development are not well harmonized. Can they be harmonized to make technology safer in the near future?

A : I don't believe the basic problems are technological. I see the opening words of the chairman of the inquiry into the Challenger disaster as the key. When the investigation began, the chairman's opening statement was that "NASA[5] had a flawed decision system." I think that is the crux of the matter.[6] It is not so much the hardware, but the decision methods we use.[7] The idea of putting giant nuclear reactors outside major population centers has always seemed to me wrong. The dangers of nuclear disaster have always been present, in my opinion.

Many technologies have dangers associated with them.[8] We are having a big

---

1) regional arrangements : 「(SEATO. CENTO등)지역방위체제」
2) geopolitical picture : 「지정학적인 양상」
3) rule out : 「배제하다」
4) expound more on : 「자세히 설명하다」
5) NASA : 「미국 항공우주국(National Aeronautics and Space Administration)」
6) the crux of the matter : 「문제의 핵심」
7) It is not so ~ methods we use : 원인은 hardware 에 있기보다는 우리가 사용하는 결정방법에 있다.
8) dangers associated with them : 「많은 기술에 관련된 위험」

discussion now about how to deal with genetic engineering.[1] This field has the promise, in my opinion, of helping to feed a hungry world and making the agriculture of the future incredibly more productive. Yet, we still don't understand. It needs regulation.

So I am not an advocate of unbridled technological development.[2] The appropriateness of technologies must be considered. Then, the basic problems are the political and economic pressures, decisional inefficiencies are pressures leading to these disasters.

Q : What scenario do you see for the information society? I mean, do we face a long development or a brief development? What role will individual behavior play in this?

A : I think movement toward what we call "an information society" is very rapid. I myself don't like that term, or terms like the communication age, the information society, the space age, etc. Not because they're wrong, but because they tend to focus on one dimension[3] of a social change that is really multi-dimensional. We're not just moving toward an information society, we're also changing the family structure. We're not seeing change only in the family structure, we're also moving toward changed social institutions and other institutions. So the change that's rolling over all of our countries, taking different forms in different places, is a massive civilizational change, I think. It affects how we think; it affects how we interrelate, and so on.

I find the information dimension extremely interesting. The question is, why an information revolution now? Why not 50 years ago, or 30 years from now? I believe the reason for the information explosion is precisely what I call demassification.[4] The units of society are becoming more multiple and more complex as the diversity of the social system increases, the society's institutions must exchange much more

1) genetic engineering : 「유전공학」
2) unbridled technological development : 「고삐 풀린 듯한 무제한의 기술의 발전」
3) on one dimension : 「(여러차원 중)한 차원에」
4) demassification : 「탈(脫)대량화」

information than before in order to operate or have any equilibrium at all.[1]

The result : The filing cabinets and the dossiers[2] begin to explode. Soon nobody can manage it. Then, somebody comes along and says, "I have a technology that can help you do this. It's called the computer, and telecommunications. That is supposed to help us manage the mass of information which the society now needs.

Of course, what happens is that computers and telecommunications make society more complex and generate even more information.

So, we're in a positive feedback loop,[3] which is creating more and more information; and we're drowning in it. In the next 20 or 30 years, we will see information and communication issues move to the center of political life — not just issues of privacy, secrets, espionage, business intelligence, but also international questions. We already have conflicts between countries over transborder data flow,[4] the parking spaces for satellites, etc. I see such questions becoming more central to political life.

The issue of what happens to the individual is not predetermined, nor inevitable. Technology doesn't demand that a certain social structure emerge ; it's a consequence of the decisions we make. If we're stupid, we can polarize our societies into people who are computer literate, have cable television, use direct broadcast satellite, and some mass of proletarians who are cut off from the information of the society. We would have the info-rich[5] and the info-poor. It would be tragic for our societies.

Q : Do you believe in God? If you do, how do you relate your belief in God to the advancement of technology?

A : I do not believe in a conventional God.

---

1) at all : 「조금이라도」
2) dossiers[dɔ́ːsiər] : 「(어떤 문제.인물에 관한)서류 일체」
3) feedback loop : 「피드백의 연쇄체제」
4) transborder data flow : 「국경 밖으로의 정보 자료 유출」
5) info-rich=information-rich : 「정보가 풍부한」

I believe I am part of a chain of human existence, that we are essentially tiny fragments of protoplasm[1] lit by a flickering of consciousness, that we link to 80, 000 million people before us and, hopefully,[2] to many millions in the future, and that we have a role to play in that. That is a kind of ethical and moral view of our position in a very big universe, wherein we are a very small species.

As to how the new technologies relate to the spread of religion, I think there will be tremendous interplay between them. For example, a recent French novel has a scenario in which the Vatican puts up its own satellite in collusion with[3] the CIA to carry out this or that ideological campaign. There is another use. If I am correct about the future of communcations — that the channels of communication are multiplying, and we will see people getting different messages through various media — that tell me we're likely to see a proliferation of different belief systems, a fragmentation of the large mass religious movements in the West, particularly as these new technologies come into play.[4] In the United States, some religious organizations have been the most sophisticated users of satellite broadcasting, such as the *Christian Broadcast Network*.

I think we also run the risk of[5] a world polarized not by East-West divisions, but by religious divisions as in the relationship of Islam to the West. It is extremely important that we work against that kind of a world. We must think about how Buddhism and other large religions with hundreds of millions of members interact on the face of the planet, for religion will remain a very important factor in people's sense of who they are and in their sense of fulfillment and purpose in life.

---

1) protoplasm : 「원형질」
2) hopefully : 「바라건대」
3) in collusion with～ : 「～와 유착하여」
4) come into play : 「작동하기 시작하다」
5) run the risk of : 「위험을 안고 있다」

10. The Heartless Lovers of Humankind

By *Paul Johnson*

I believe the reflective portion of mankind[1] is divided into two groups: those who are interested in people and care about them : and those who are interested in ideas. The first group forms the pragmatistes and tends to make the best statesmen.[2] The second is the intellectuals; and if their attachment to ideas is passionate, and not only passonate but programmatic,[3] they are almost certain to abuse whatever power they acquire. For, instead of allowing their ideas of government to emerge from people, shaped by observation of how people actually behave and what they really desire, intellectuals reverse the process, deducing[4] their ideas first from principle and then seeking to impose them on living men and women.

In the past 200 years the influence of intellectuals has grown steadily. It has always been there, of course, for in their earlier incarnations[5] as priests, scribes[6] and soothsayers,[7] intellectuals have laid claim to[8] guide society from the very beginning. From the time of Voltaire and Rousseau, the secular intellectual has filled the

---

1) the reflective portion of mankind : ~ 인류 가운데 생각이 깊은 사람들
2) to make the best statesmen. : make 는 되다, ~구성하다
3) programmatic : ~ 계획적인
4) deducing : 연역하다 cf. induct 귀납하다.
5) incarnations ~ : 구체적으로 드러난 존재
6) scribes ~ 〔성서〕 : 유대의 율법학자, 필경사
7) soothsayer ~ : 예언자, 점장이
8) laid claim to ~ : ~할 자격이 있다고 주장하다.

position left by the decline of the cleric,[1] and is proving more arrogant, permanent and above all dangerous than his clerical version.[2]

Almost all intellectuals profess to[3] love humanity and to be working for its improvement and happiness. But it is the idea of humanity they love, rather than the actual individuals who compose it. They love humanity-in-general,[4] rather than men-and women-in-particular. [5]

Insensitivity to the needs and views of other people is, indeed, a characteristic of those passionately concerned with ideas. For their primary focus of attention is, naturally, with the evolution of those ideas in their own heads; they become, in the full sense, egocentric.[6] The intellectual's indefference or hostility is not directed merely toward those who do not fit into his schemes[7] for humanity-in-general but also toward those in his own circle who, for one reason or another, refuse to play their allotted roles in his own life.

In the 20th century, building upon[8] 19th century foundations, the appetite for violence in the pursuit and realization of ideas has become the original sin of the intellectual. Consider, for instance, the repeated expression of admiration by intellectuals for ruthless men of action,[9] and their long succession of violent heroes : Stalin, Mao Tse-tung, Castro, Ho Chi Minh.

Intellectuals occasionally demur at[10] the quantity of the slaughter, the sheer number[11] of the "necessary murders"; they nearly always have accepted the principle

---

1) the cleric : ~ 성직자
2) his clerical version : 그의 맞상대인 성직자
3) profess to : ~ 공언하다. 여기서 professor(교수)가 생겼다.
4) humanity-in-general : 인류 전체
5) men-and-women-in-particular : 특정한 남녀
6) egocentric : 자기자신이 모든 경험의 중심, 목적, 규범이라는 견해를 가지고 생각하거나 행동하는 것
7) schemes : ~ 구상, 체계
8) building upon : ~ = relying upon
9) men of action : ~ 행동가, 실천가
10) demur at : ~ 에 의의를 제기하다, 반대하다.
11) the sheer number : 더도말고 그대로의 수(자)

that socialist utopias must, if necessary, be erected on violent foundations.

While the armchair men of violence[1] in the West applauded and condoned, intellectuals elsewhere participated and often directed the great slaughters of modern times. Many helped to create the Cheka, the progenitor[2] of the present KGB. Intellectuals were prominent at all stages in the events leading up to the Nazi holocaust. The events in Cambodia in the 1970s, in which between one-fifth and one-third of the nation[3] was starved to death or murdered, were entirely the work of a group of intellectuals, who were for the most part pupils and admirers of Jean-Paúl Sartre — "Sartre's Children," as I call them.

Wherever men and regimes seek to impose ideas on people, wherever the inhuman process of social engineering is set in motion[4] — shoveling flesh and blood around as though it were soil of concrete — there you will find intellectuals in plenty. Pushing people around is the characteristic activity of all forms of socialism, whether Soviet socialism, or German National Socialism, or , for instance, the peculiar form of ethnic socialism, known as apartheid,[5] we find in South Africa; that sinister set of ideas, it is worth noting, was wholly the invention of intellectuals cobbled together[6] in the social psychology department of Stellenbosch University. Other African totalitarian ideologies are likewise the work of local intellectuals, usually sociologists.

So one of the lessons of our century is : Beware the intellectuals. Not merely should they be kept well away from the levers of power, they also should be objects of peculiar suspicion when they seek to offer collective advice.

Beware committees, conferences, leagues of intellectuals! For intellectuals, far

---

1) armchair men of violence : 이론상으로만 폭력을 지지하는(휘두르는)사람
2) progenitor : ~ 원조, 조상
3) between one-fifth and one-third of ~ : 문장의 주어
4) set in motion : ~ 을 가동시키다.
5) apartheid ~ : 〔민족 격리정책, 특히 남아 공화국의 흑인 또는 기타 유색인종에 대한〕 인종차별정책
6) cobbled together : 날림으로 만들다, 급조하다.

from being highly individualistic and nonconformist people, are in fact ultraconformist within the circles formed by those whose approval they seek and value. This is what makes them, en masse,[1] so dangerous, because it enables them to create cultural climates, which themselves often generate irrational, violent and tragic courses of action.

Remember at all times, that people must always come before ideas and not the other way around.[2]

---

1) en masse : ~ 한무더기로. (in a mass)
2) the other way around [about or round] ~ : 반대로, 거꾸로

11. The Unromantic Generation

By *Bruce Webber*

Here is a contemporary[1] love story. Twenty-four-year-old, Clark Wolfsberger, a native of St. Louis, and Kim[2] Wright, 25, who is from Chicago, live in Dallas. They've been going together[3] since they met as students at Southern Methodist University three years ago. They are an attractive pair, trim[4] and athletic, she dark and lissome,[5] he broad shouldered and square-jawed. They have jobs they took immediately after graduating — Clark works at Talent Sports International, a sports marketing and management company ; Kim is an assistant account executive[6] at Tracy-Locke, a large advertising agency — and they are in love.

"We're very compatible,[7] she says.

"We don't need much time together to confirm our relationship, he says.

When they speak about the future, they hit the two-career family[8] notes[9] that are conventional now in the generations ahead of them.

"At 30, I'll probably be married and planning a family, says Kim.

---

1) contemporary : 「동시대의 . 현대판의」
2) Kim : a male or female given name
3) go together : 「애인 사이이다」
4) trim : 「균형잡힌」
5) lissome : 「날씬한」
6) assistant account executive : 「(항공회사 등의) 섭외부 차장」
7) compatible : 「마음이 맞는」
8) two-career family : 「맞벌이 가정(double-income family)」
9) hit ~ notes : 「~라는 투로 말하다」

"I'll stay in advertising. I'll be a late parent. "

"By 30, I'll definitely be married ; either that or waterskiing naked in Monaco", Clark says, laughing. "No, I'll be married. Well established[1] in my line of work.[2] Have the home, have the dog. Maybe not a kid yet, but eventually. I'm definitely in favor of kids."

In the month I spent last winter visiting several cities around the country, interviewing recent college graduates about marriage, relationships, modern romance, I heard a lot of this, life equations already written,[3] doubt banished. I undertook the trip because of the impression so many of us have; that in one wavelike rush to business school and Wall Street,[4] young Americans have succumbed to a culture of immediate gratification[5] and gone deep-down elitist on us.[6] I set out to test the image with an informal survey meant to take the emotional temperature of[7] a generation, not far behind my own, that seems so cynical, so full of such "material"[8] girls and boys.

The 60 or so people I interviewed, between the ages of 22 and 26, were a diverse group. They spoke in distinct voices, testifying to[9] a range of political and social views. Graduate students, lawyers, teachers, entertainers, business people, they are pursuing a variety of interests. What they have in common is that they graduated from college, are living in or around an urban center and are heterosexual,[10] mirrors of myself when I graduated from college in 1975.

And yet, as I moved from place to place, another quality emerged to the degree that I'd call it characteristic:They are planners.[11] It was the one thing that surprised

1) well established : 「기반이 잡힌」
2) line of work : 「직업」
3) life equations already written : 「인생에 관한 갖가지 질문이 이미 해답을 본」
4) Wall Street : 「미국의 금융계」
5) immediate gratification : 「즉각적인 만족」
6) go deep down elitist on us : 「(우리 보기에)자못 엘리트적이다」
7) take the emotional temperature of : 「~의 감정적 체온(질)을 재다」
8) material : 「물질적인, 타산적인」
9) testify to : 「입증하다」
10) heterosexual : 「이성애의」 cf. homosexual
11) planners : 「계획을 세워 행동하는 사람」

me, this looking ahead with certainty.[1)] They have priorities. I'd ask about love; they'd give me a graph.[2)]

They are not heartless, soulless, cold or unimaginative. They are self-preoccupied[3)] but that's a quality, it seems to me, for which youthful generations have always been known. What distinguishes this generation from mine, I think, is that they're aware of it. They have come of age,[4)] of course, at a time when American social traditions barely survive. Since 1975 there have been more than a million divorces annually, and it is well publicized that nearly half of all marriages now end in divorce. Yet the era of condoned casual promiscuity[5)] and sexual experimentation — itself once an undermining of the nation's social fabric[6)] — now seems to be drawing to a close[7)] with the ever-spreading plague of sexually transmitted disease.[8)]

The achievements of feminist activism[9)] — particularly the infusion of women into the work force — have altered the expectations that the sexes[10)] — have for each other and themselves.

And finally, the new college graduates have been weaned on[11)] scarifying forecasts of economic gloom.[12)] They feel housing problems already ; according to *American Demographics* magazine, the proportion of young people living at home with their parents was higher in 1985 than in the last three censuses. They're aware, too, of predictions that however affluent they are themselves, they're probably better off[13)] than their children will be.

---

1) this looking ahead with certainty : 「확신에 찬 전망」
2) they'd ～ a graph : 「사랑에 관해서 물으면 도표를 내밀 것이다」(I'd ask～)
3) self-preoccupied : 「자기 일에만 골몰하는」
4) come of age : 「성년이 되다」
5) the era of ～ promiscuity : 「난잡한 성관계를 눈감아 주던 시대」
6) social fabric : 「사회체제」
7) draw to a close : 「끝이 가까워지다」
8) sexually transmitted disease : 「성병」 약칭 STD.
9) feminist activism : 「여성(권)운동」
10) the sexes : 「남성과 여성」
11) weaned on : 「이유(離乳)시키다」
12) scarifying forecasts of economic gloom : 「경기침체에 대한 암울한 전망 속에」
13) better off : 「더 부유한」 of well off

With all this in mind, today's graduates seem keenly aware that the future is bereft of[1] conventional expectations, that what's ahead is more chaotic than mysterious. I've come to think it ironic that in a youth-minded culture such as ours, one that ostensibly[2] grants greater freedom of choice to young people than it ever has before, those I spoke with seem largely restrained. Concerned with,[3] if not consumed by, narrowing the options down,[4] getting on track, they are aiming already at a distant comfort and security.

Micah Materre, 25, recently completed an internship[5] at *CBS News* in Chicago and is looking for a job in broadcast jouralism. Like many of the young people I talked to, she is farsighted in her romantic outlook : "I went out with[6] a guy last fall. He had a good job as a stockbroker. He was nice to me. But then he started telling me about his family. And there were problems. And I thought, "What happens if I fall in love and we get married? What then?"

The prevalent notion is that chemistry is untrustworthy;[7] parents need to be up to snuff[8] according to pretty rigorous standards.[9] Ellen Lubin, 26, of Los Angeles, for example, has just gotten engaged to the man she has been living with for two years. When she met him, she says:"I wasn't that attracted to him right away. But there were things about him that made me say, 'This is what I want in a man. 'He's bright. He's a go-getter.[10] He was making tons of money at the age of 25. He's well-connected.[11] He was like my mentor in coming to deal with life in the city. "

Today's graduates have forged a new attitude entirely. In spite of the high divorce

---

1) is bereft of : 「빼앗긴, 잃은」
2) ostensibly : 「(겉보기에)~ 한 듯한」
3) concerned with : 「열심인」
4) narrowing~down : 「방향(진로)을 설정하다」
5) internship : 「수습(기간)」
6) went out with : 「사귀다」
7) chemistry is untrustworthy : 「감정을 믿을 수 없다」
8) up to snuff : 「만족할 만하다」
9) pretty rigorous standards : 「꽤 까다로운 기준」
10) go-getter : 「수완가」
11) well-connected : 「집안이 좋은, 대인관계가 좋은」

rate, many of those I spoke with have marriage in mind. Overwhelmingly, they see it as not only desirable, but inevitable. Because of the odds,[1] they approach it with wariness[2] and pragmatism. More cautious than their parents (for American men in 1985, the median age at the time of their first marriage was 25. 5, the highest since the turn of the century; it was 23. 3 for women, a record), they are methodical[3] in comparison with me.

Perhaps that explains why I find the way they speak about marriage so unromantic. Men and women tend to couch their views in[4] different terms, but they seem to share the perception that marriage is necessarily restricting.

Nonetheless,[5] they trust in its rewards, whatever they are. Overall, it doesn't represent the kind of commitment that seems viable without adequate preparation.

"I've been dating someone for a year and a half, "says Tom Grossman, a-24-year-old graduate of the University of Texas. "We don't talk about marriage, and frankly I don't think it'll occur. Currently area sales manager in San Antonio for the John H. Harland Co. , a check well-off[6] financially, and I don't want that struggle to interfere with the marriage. There are too many other stress factors involved. I want to be able to enjoy myself right away. And I never want to look back and think that if I hadn't gotten married, I could have accomplished more".

According to annual surveys of 300,000 college freshmen conducted by the Higher Education Research Institute at the Graduate School of Education of the University of California at Los Angeles, young people today, by the time they enter college, are more inclined to express concrete life objectives than they've been for many years. Of those surveyed last fall, 73. 2percent cited being "very well-off financially" as an essential or very important objective. That's up from 63. 3 percent

---

1) the odds : 「확률」여기서는 높은 이혼율.
2) wariness : 「신중함」
3) methodical : 「체계적인」
4) couch their views in : 「견해를 표명하다」
5) Nonetheless : 「그럼에도 불구하고」
6) a check-well-off : 「잘 사는 사람」 well-off 항에 대답한 사람.

in 1980, 49. 5 percent in 1975. At the same time, the percentage of freshmen who consider it important to "develop a meaningful philosophy of life"has declined from 64. 2percent in 1975 to 40. 6 percent last year.

Many of the people I spoke to feel the pressure of peer scrutiny.[1] A status thing has evolved, to which many seem to have regretfully succumbed. Several expressed a weariness with meeting someone new and having to present themselves by their credentials.[2] Yet, over-whelmingly, asked what they're looking for in a romantic partner, they responded first with phrases such as "an educated professional" and "someone with directions." They've conceded, more or less consciously, that unenlightened and exclusionary as it is,[3] it's very uncool[4] not to know what you want and not to be already chasing it.

---

1) peer scrutiny : 「동료들의 평가(주시)」
2) credentials : 「학력, 경력 등 자신을 내놓을 수 있는 것」
3) exclusionary as it is : 「배타적인 것이기는 하나」
4) uncool : 「바람직하지 않은, 모양이 좋지 않은」

편저자

김용권
서강대학교 영문과 교수 역임
서강대학교 명예교수

조성규
연세대학교 영문과 교수 역임
연세대학교 명예교수

김명렬
서울대학교 영문과 교수 역임
서울대학교 명예교수

Current English Two

초판 1쇄 발행 _ 1993년 8월 15일
초판 6쇄 발행 _ 2012년 8월 30일

편 저 자 • 김용권, 조성규, 김명렬
발 행 인 • 정 현 걸
발　　행 • 신 아 사
인　　쇄 • 예지인쇄
출판등록 • 1956년 1월 5일 (제9-52호)
주　　소 • 서울특별시 은평구 녹번동 28-36번지 2F
전　　화 • (02)382-6411 · 팩스 (02)382-6401
홈페이지 • www.shinasa.co.kr
E - MAIL • shinasa@chol.com

ISBN 89-8396-001-9 (93740)

정가 10,000원